1 CORINTHIANS
A SELF-STUDY GUIDE

Irving L. Jensen

MOODY PRESS
CHICAGO

ISBN: 0-8024-4467-9

1 2 3 4 5 6 7 Printing/EP/Year 94 93 92 91 90

Printed in the United States of America

Contents

Introduction

Problems are to be found in all Christian churches, and there are no exceptions. Wherever the human dimension is involved, corruption is present.

Christians can and do sin because they have not yet been delivered of that old sinful nature, which wars against their new nature received at the new birth. So the setting of a local church includes the stark reality of a spiritual warfare between evil and righteousness. Two main values of studying 1 Corinthians are in seeing God's diagnosis of our own spiritual maladies and in learning His prescriptions for cure. The Holy Spirit would not have inspired Paul to write this letter to the Corinthian church, which was plagued with problems, if there was no hope for its recovery. May we enter into a study of the letter with strong faith that God can help us too.

Suggestions for Study

Basic Bible study in the mother tongue should be direct, personal, unencumbered with technicalities, and practical. If it is all these, it will also be inspiring and thoroughly enjoyable.

The study suggestions given below follow procedures that are consistently applied in the manuals of this self-study series.

1. Spend most of your time with the Bible text itself. Don't read into the text any meaning that is not there.

2. Let context—the surrounding words and phrases—be your ally in interpreting any particular passage.

3. Train your eyes—physical and spiritual—to keep seeing things in the text. Don't be content with a casual, quick glance. Comprehensive analysis can be the most enjoyable part of your study.

4. Compare modern versions with the King James Version reading for help in determining the full meaning of a word or phrase.

5. Be continually on the lookout for spiritual lessons taught in the passage. These would involve your relation to God and to other people, commands to obey, sins to confess and avoid, promises to claim, paths to pursue, warnings to heed.

6. Charts appear throughout this manual, as they do in the entire self-study series. This emphasizes the importance of the "eye gate" in Bible study. Some charts are given in full, as background and guide for your study. Most of the charts are only partially completed; your writing down observations on these should open up many new insights into this wonderful book of God. You may want to use standard size paper (8 1/2 x 11") for such work sheets. Pastors and Bible teachers who have access to an overhead projector can use charts to great advantage in their meetings. (Some pastors work with overhead projectors at their Sunday night and midweek services.)

7. This manual is divided into fourteen lessons. Some lessons, because of their length, should be studied in more than one study unit. You should decide how long each study unit should be. Depth, not area, and relaxation, not pressure, are the determining guides here.

8. Study the Bible text prayerfully and carefully. Be convinced that the one who inspired the Scriptures—the Holy Spirit Himself—wants your study to be fruitful and will offer you all the illumination needed to make it so.

Suggestions for Leaders of Bible Classes

1. Make clear to the class members what you want them to do in preparation for the next meeting. Encourage them to write out answers to all questions and to record observations on analytical charts when these are called for.

2. Stimulate discussion during the class meeting. Encourage everyone to ask questions as well as share answers. Some can do more, some can do less, but all can do some. Never embarrass a member of your class in any aspect of discussion.

3. Recognize difficult passages in the Bible when they appear. Use these occasions to emphasize the maxim of interpretation that *whatever is essential is clear*.

4. If possible reproduce the charts of the manual on a chalkboard or with the aid of an overhead projector. This will help unify your lesson and provide constant reference to surrounding context.

5. Devote the last part of each meeting to sharing the spiritual lessons taught by the Scripture passage. This should be the climax of the class hour.

Lesson 1
Background

It is no exaggeration to say that ancient Corinth was similar to today's large American cities. It was a busy, cosmopolitan, commercial center known by all. The first Christian church of Corinth had an equally strong likeness to many urban churches of today. As you study this lesson try to *visualize* the setting of Paul's first letter to the Corinthian church. In doing so you will find it easy and natural to apply its teachings to the twentieth century. Assuredly the letter was written not only for a local congregation of one generation but for Christians everywhere throughout the entire Christian age.

I. CORINTH: THE CITY AND ITS PEOPLE

When Paul visited Corinth for the first time in A.D. 50, he must have been impressed by its stately buildings and bustling commerce. This Greek city was widely acclaimed as the hub of the Roman Empire's commerce, a strategic position that Paul no doubt coveted for the advantage of propagating the gospel of Jesus Christ.

The following descriptions will help you appreciate what Paul saw, learned, and experienced concerning the city and its people.

A. Name

The Greek name *Korintos* means "ornament."

B. Geography

Observe on the map the strategic location of Corinth on the four-mile-wide isthmus between the Ionian and Aegean seas. Shippers moving cargo between Italy and Asia Minor via Corinth avoided the dangerous voyage around the southern tip of Greece. Small ships were moved across the isthmus by tramway, or cargo of the larger ships was transferred to transports waiting at the eastern port.[1]

**GEOGRAPHY OF CORINTH,
SHOWING CORINTHIAN GULF AND CANAL**

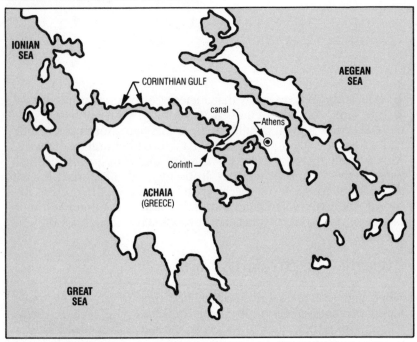

C. History

Corinth's ancient history revolves around two events: (1) the destruction of the old city by the Roman general Mummius, 146 B.C., and (2) the rebuilding of the city by Julius Caesar, with its gaining status as a Roman colony, 46 B.C. How old, then, was the new city when Paul first visited it?

1. For an excellent description of the sights that Paul probably saw on his first visit to Corinth, consult Charles F. Pfeiffer and Howard F. Vos, *The Wycliffe Historical Geography of Bible Lands* (Chicago: Moody, 1967), pp. 477-87.

D. Population

Estimates of size in Paul's day vary from 100,000 to 700,000. There was a mixture of races (Roman, Greek, oriental) and a large distribution of mobile-type occupations (e.g., sailors and businessmen). A large proportion of its population was composed of slaves.

E. Political Status

Corinth was a Roman colony, the capital of the province of Achaia. Gallio was proconsul ("deputy," KJV*) of the province during Paul's visit (Acts 18:12).

F. Moral Condition

The depraved character of the old city of Corinth, exemplified by prostitute priestesses serving in the temple of Aphrodite,[2] goddess of beauty and love, was carried over into the new city of New Testament times. The very word *Korinthiazomai* ("to act the Corinthian") came to mean "to commit fornication." One writer has described Corinth as "a seaman's paradise, a drunkard's heaven, and a virtuous woman's hell."[3]

G. Activities

1. *Commerce.* Movement of shipping across the isthmus was Corinth's number one business. Some of its own manufactured products included items of pottery and brass.
2. *Education.* Study of arts and science flourished. There were studios of language and schools of philosophy. Yet Paul, raised in the environment of the university of Tarsus, and trained under the great teacher Gamaliel, was keen to detect an intellectualism that was both smug and superficial. (Read some of Paul's references to knowledge and wisdom in such passages as 1:20-21, 27; 2:1-8.)
3. *Sports.* Corinth was a famous sports center, hosting the Isthmian Games (similar in some ways to the Olympics) held every two years. It is interesting to observe that corruption in sports

*King James Version.
2. This Greek goddess was identified with the Roman goddess Venus.
3. Joseph M. Gettys, *How to Study I Corinthians* (Richmond: John Knox, 1951), p. 10.

9

events was widespread at this time.[4] (Read Paul's references to sports in 9:24-27.)

4. *Religion*. Corinth was a city of many gods and various cults. Judaism was one of its oriental religions. The Jews' synagogue was Paul's favorite place of contact for reaching people with the gospel when he first arrived in Corinth (Acts 18:1-4).

II. THE ARRIVAL OF PAUL THE EVANGELIST-TEACHER

Read Acts 18:1-18*a* for the historical record of Paul's first evangelistic ministry in Corinth. This visit took place on the apostle's second missionary journey about A.D. 50. Answer the following questions on the basis of the Bible text.

1. Does the text indicate when Aquila and Priscilla were converted to Christ? Read these other New Testament references to this couple, and try to decide when they may have become believers (if they were not already believers when Paul first met them, Acts 18:2). Acts 18:18*b*, 26; Romans 16:3; 1 Corinthians 16:19; 2 Timothy 4:19.

2. What different verbs of the Acts passage are used to describe Paul's *word* ministry (e.g., "reasoned," v. 4)?

3. To what different groups did Paul minister?

4. What were the different reactions to Paul's message?

How many conversions were there?

5. Account for Paul's action of verse 6.

4. Pfeiffer and Vos, p. 485.

10

6. What does this passage teach about revelation and divine help?

_____

_____

_____

7. What do you think constituted Paul's "teaching the word of God" (18:11)?

_____

_____

_____

8. What is suggested by the words "And Paul . . . tarried there yet a good while" (18:18*a*)?

_____

_____

9. One of the important things Paul did while in Corinth was to write the two epistles to the Thessalonians.[5] Read 2 Thessalonians 3:1-2 for references to Paul's ministry at Corinth at this time. (Cf.1 Thess. 2:15.)

III. THE FIRST CHURCH OF CORINTH

Our analytical study of Paul's first letter to the Corinthians will reveal much about the spiritual condition of this church, so that need not be mentioned here. Other observations include the following:

1. The organized church began around A.D. 50 as a small nucleus of believers, most of whom were Gentiles (e.g., Justus, Acts 18:7), and some of whom were Jews (e.g., Crispus, Acts 18:8). Their meeting place from the start may have been an upper chamber of the house of one of the group, such as Crispus.

2. Most of the members were probably of the poorer or middle-class strata (cf. 1 Cor. 1:26ff., which only suggests this observation).

3. The church members were slow to mature in their Christian faith and conduct (cf. 3:1ff.). This was part of the heavy burden borne by Paul, which he referred to as "the care of all the churches" (2 Cor. 11:28).

---

5. There was probably an interim of a few months between the writings of the two epistles.

11

4. Apollos was the church's pastor-teacher for part of the time between Paul's second and third missionary journeys. (Read Acts 18:24–19:1. Also read the seven references to Apollos in 1 Cor. 1:12; 3:4-6, 22; 4:6; 16:12. The last reference concerns a proposed second tour of duty by Apollos in Corinth.)

5. First Corinthians 1:12 and 9:5 only suggest the *possibility* that Peter may have ministered to the church at Corinth.

IV. CONTACTS AFTER THE FIRST VISIT
AND BEFORE THE FIRST EPISTLE

Two possible contacts that Paul had with the Corinthian converts after his first visit and before writing 1 Corinthians were these.[6]

1. A short visit to combat an incipient opposition to the apostle's ministry and to correct other evils. Apparently his mission was not effective.[7] (Read 2 Cor. 2:1; 12:14; 13:1-2. Note the reference to a forthcoming "third time" visit.)

2. A letter referred to in 1 Corinthians 5:9. At least part of the letter was written to correct existing evils in the church. The letter is not part of the New Testament canon and was therefore not divinely inspired Scripture.[8]

V. THE FIRST INSPIRED EPISTLE TO THE CORINTHIANS

This is the book on which we will focus our attention for the remainder of this study manual.

A. Time and Place Written

Paul wrote this letter on his third missionary journey, toward the end of his three-year ministry in the city of Ephesus (1 Cor. 16:8)[9]

---

6. Different views are held on this obscure subject, because of the relative silence of the New Testament. You may want to consult various authors for a full discussion. Concerning your study of the inspired epistles to the Corinthians, rest confidently in the principle that one's study of what God has chosen to reveal is not jeopardized by His *silence* concerning any subject.

7. This unrecorded visit is placed before 1 Corinthians by A. Robertson and A. Plummer, *First Epistle of St. Paul to the Corinthians* (Edinburgh: T. & T. Clark, 1911), pp. xxi-xxv, and by Henry Alford, *The Greek Testament* (Chicago: Moody, 1958), 2:52-54. The visit is placed *after* 1 Corinthians by Merrill Tenney, *New Testament Survey* (Grand Rapids: Eerdmans, 1953), p. 298, and by S. Lewis Johnson, "First Corinthians," in *The Wycliffe Bible Commentary*, p. 1228.

8. Paul obviously wrote many letters in his lifetime besides those that were inspired.

9. See Acts 20:31; cf. 19:8, 10 for the time element.

12

The year of writing was A.D. 55. Read Acts 19:1-20 for a description of the fruitful work he was doing at Ephesus in the power of God, while *in absentia* he was trying to help the Corinthian church with its problems.

B. Occasion

Paul was a traveling evangelist who took to heart the follow-up work of nurturing the young converts he had led to Christ. As noted earlier, he called this burden "the care of all the churches" (2 Cor. 11:28). Paul learned of the Corinthians' problems through reports (see 1: 11 and 5:1) and inquiries (7:1, 25; 8:1; 11:2; 12:1; 15:1; 16:1) originating with members and leaders of the church (cf. 1 Cor. 16:17.) If he had already made a short visit since founding the church, he knew of some of the problems firsthand as well.

C. Purposes

Among Paul's purposes in writing were these: (1) to identify the basic problems underlying the reports and inquiries, (2) to offer solutions by way of doctrine and example, (3) to give extended teaching on related doctrines, (4) to give at least a short defense of his apostleship, and (5) to exhort the believers in the ways of a full, mature Christian life. More will be said about these purposes in Lesson 2 (survey). How do they suggest the title, assigned by one writer, "The Epistle of Sanctification"?

D. Authenticity

First Corinthians is one of the best-attested epistles as to authorship and unity of content.

E. Relation to the Other New Testament Books

The location of the Corinthian letters in the New Testament canon is a natural one when one considers *general emphases*.[10] This is shown in the following diagram:

---

10. This observation holds only in the large overall sense. For example, there is much interpretation in the gospels and Acts, just as there is much application in Romans and much interpretation in the Corinthian letters.

13

THE GOSPEL OF JESUS CHRIST

NEW TESTAMENT ORDER	EMPHASES
GOSPELS ACTS	HISTORICAL FACTS
ROMANS	INTERPRETATIONS
1 and 2 CORINTHIANS	APPLICATIONS

Chart A shows all twenty-seven books of the New Testament grouped according to topic. Note that the Corinthian letters are classified under the heading *Ecclesiology* (doctrine of the church). Second Corinthians (Paul's Ministry Vindicated) is more personal than 1 Corinthians, just as 2 Timothy (Paul's Ministry Accomplished) is more personal than 1 Timothy.

VI. APPLYING 1 CORINTHIANS TO TODAY

It is not difficult to apply 1 Corinthians to our own lives, because it is such a practical epistle throughout. G. Campbell Morgan's appeal concerning a study of the book is appropriate:

> Think of it . . . not merely as addressed to a city of long ago, today lost comparatively and in ruins, with all its splendor gone, but as addressed to a church there, and to all who in every place call upon the name of our Lord Jesus Christ. THIS LETTER IS TO US.[11]

The few questions given below emphasize this practical application.
1. In what ways was Corinth of Paul's day like many cities today?

_____

_____

2. On the basis of what you know about Corinth, relate the following two statements to each other: (1) a classic New Testament passage on the doctrine of sin is found in Romans (1:18–3:20); (2) Paul wrote Romans from Corinth.[12]

_____

_____

11. G. Campbell Morgan, *The Corinthian Letters of Paul*, p. 10. Emphasis supplied.
12. On his third missionary journey.

14

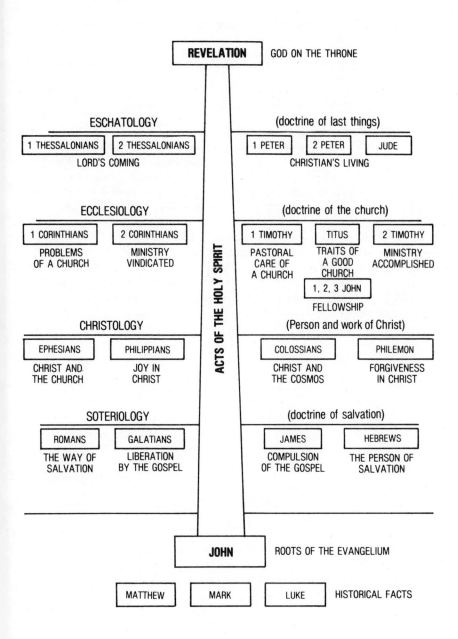

REVELATION — GOD ON THE THRONE

ESCHATOLOGY — (doctrine of last things)

1 THESSALONIANS	2 THESSALONIANS

LORD'S COMING

1 PETER	2 PETER	JUDE

CHRISTIAN'S LIVING

ECCLESIOLOGY — (doctrine of the church)

1 CORINTHIANS	2 CORINTHIANS

PROBLEMS OF A CHURCH — MINISTRY VINDICATED

1 TIMOTHY	TITUS	2 TIMOTHY

PASTORAL CARE OF A CHURCH — TRAITS OF A GOOD CHURCH — MINISTRY ACCOMPLISHED

1, 2, 3 JOHN

FELLOWSHIP

CHRISTOLOGY — (Person and work of Christ)

EPHESIANS	PHILIPPIANS

CHRIST AND THE CHURCH — JOY IN CHRIST

COLOSSIANS	PHILEMON

CHRIST AND THE COSMOS — FORGIVENESS IN CHRIST

SOTERIOLOGY — (doctrine of salvation)

ROMANS	GALATIANS

THE WAY OF SALVATION — LIBERATION BY THE GOSPEL

JAMES	HEBREWS

COMPULSION OF THE GOSPEL — THE PERSON OF SALVATION

ACTS OF THE HOLY SPIRIT

JOHN — ROOTS OF THE EVANGELIUM

MATTHEW	MARK	LUKE

HISTORICAL FACTS

3. How do you account for the successes of Paul's ministry in Corinth on his first visit there?

_____

_____

Consider the following comments of one writer.

> The conditions which Paul and the Christian gospel faced in Corinth should give pause to the modern preacher who laments the moral corruption of his own day and feels that his task is almost impossible in such a context. Conditions in Corinth were far worse. The message and power of the gospel are the same in the twentieth century as they were in the first.[13]

4. What do you think contributes to spiritual problems in the early months and years of a born-again believer? Why do spiritual problems often arise very early in the life of a newly organized local church? (Answering these questions is a good introduction to the next lesson, where various problems will be viewed, at least in a general way.)

13. Pfeiffer and Vos, p. 481.

Lesson 2
Survey

Picture the whole: then analyze the parts—that is the correct procedure for study of a Bible book. This lesson, therefore, is devoted to a survey, or skyscraper view, of 1 Corinthians. In such a study you may expect to gain (1) an overall *perspective*, of such things as atmosphere and movement, (2) a general idea of the major *emphases* of the epistle, and (3) an orientation to the surrounding *context* of each chapter, which will be analyzed beginning in Lesson 3.

There are various ways to survey a Bible book because of the "roving" character of this phase of Bible study. The suggestions given below are intended to help you see especially the highlights of 1 Corinthians as you move about the pages of the epistle. Bear in mind throughout your study that a main purpose of survey is to see the overall *pattern* or *structure* of the book. We will record this on a survey chart, about which more will be said later.

I. FIRST READING

This is the cursory, one-sitting reading of the whole epistle, intended to break the ice, launch you on your project, and give a taste of good things to come. For a fresh approach to the letter, read it as though you had never seen it before. Here are some suggestions:

1. Recall what you studied in Lesson 1 about Corinth and the Corinthian church. Visualize this possible setting: A leader of the church has called a special meeting of the congregation. You are among them. He stands to announce that messengers have just brought a long letter from Paul, which he would like to read at this time.[1] He reads, and you are there!

---

1. First Corinthians is Paul's longest epistle.

2. Try reading the epistle aloud, as though you were the reader mentioned above. It will amaze you how fresh and new the text will appear by doing this.

3. For this reading only, you may choose to use a modern paraphrase of 1 Corinthians to feel the flow and unity of the letter.[2]

4. Don't tarry over details in your reading. You will have ample time to do this in your later analytical studies.

5. When you have completed this cursory reading, reflect for a few minutes on what has impressed you. Jot down some of these impressions.

II. SECOND READING

During this second reading you should begin to *record* observations. In Bible study it is important to establish the habit of writing things down. Whether you use a notebook or separate sheets of paper, recording observations is one tangible and fruitful way to draw dividends from your investment of precious time. "A pencil is one of the best eyes."

A. Chapter Titles

Assign a chapter title to each chapter of the epistle. (A chapter title is a strong word or phrase, preferably taken from the text, intended to serve as a clue to at least one main part of the chapter.) Record your titles on a chart similar to Chart B. (Note: There are two segments in chap. 1; and 11:2 replaces 11:1 as the beginning of a new segment.)

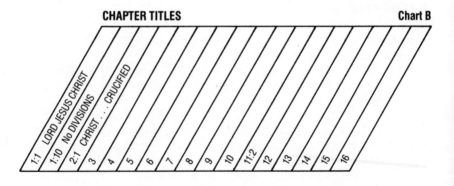

CHAPTER TITLES   **Chart B**

2. *The Living Bible* is recommended for this reading.

B. Key Words and Phrases

As you read the epistle, underline the words and phrases that strike you as being strong and important. Develop an alertness to the power of a single word in the Book of God.

III. SEARCH AND CORRELATE

You can move out in various directions in your study from this point on. Some "search missions" are suggested below. Your ultimate aim, of course, should be to correlate all your observations in one overall picture of 1 Corinthians. Look briefly at survey Chart C at this time for suggestions as to how you may want to construct your own chart of 1 Corinthians on the basis of your studies. (Note: Be sure to read every Bible reference cited below.)

1. Look for groupings of chapters according to a common subject. A clue to this is Paul's use of the phrases "It is reported" (1:11; 5:1) and "Now concerning" (7:1, 25; 8:1; 12:1; 16:1; cf. 11:2). Actually, 1 Corinthians is one of the simplest of Paul's epistles as to general structure. Justify the twofold outline shown on Chart C: Acknowledging Reports; Answering Inquiries. What kinds of problems are discussed in chapters 1-6? What kinds of questions are discussed in chapters 7-15?

2. How do 1:1-9 and 16:1-24 serve as introduction and conclusion, respectively?

3. First Corinthians is one of the most practical of all of Paul's epistles. Make a note of all the problems explicitly mentioned by Paul in the epistle. Group these according to common subject, and compare your conclusions with the outlines of Chart C.

4. Go through the epistle and mark in your Bible every block of positive doctrine, as over against the discussions of the various evils of the Corinthian church. (The length of each block will vary from a paragraph to more than a chapter.) Note also where Paul gives personal testimony.

5. What chapters could be called "golden chapters" for the particular subjects they present?

6. Write a list of key words for 1 Corinthians. Compare your list with that of Chart C.

7. In your own words, write out what you think is the theme of 1 Corinthians. From this derive a short title. Have you seen a verse in the epistle that reflects this theme and could be called a key verse?

8. What primary doctrines of the gospel appear from time to time throughout the epistle? Did you notice, for example, references to the death of Christ? (Check a concordance for the twelve

direct references to this subject in these words: blood, cross, crucified, died, sacrificed.)

9. How would you describe the *style* of this epistle? Writers have observed that it is the most varied of all of Paul's epistles, ranging from informal, conversational style to a "lofty and sustained solemnity."[3] Did you observe in your reading such literary devices as logic, poetry, narration, exposition, and the frequent use of questions? Alford describes Paul the writer with these words:

> The depths of the spiritual, the moral, the intellectual, the physical world are open to him. He summons to his aid the analogies of nature. He enters minutely into the varieties of human infirmity and prejudice. . . . He praises, reproves, exhorts, and teaches. Where he strikes, he heals. His large heart holding all, where he has grieved any, he grieves likewise; where it is in his power to give joy, he first overflows with joy himself.[4]

10. Study carefully the partially completed survey Chart C. Refer to this chart often in the course of your analytical studies of the epistle. Note that the spaces for SOLUTIONS and EXAMPLES at the bottom of the chart are left blank. Record the various solutions and examples as you observe these in your analytical studies.

TWO CONCLUDING EXERCISES

1. Make a list of all the subjects you can remember about which Paul has written in 1 Corinthians. If you are studying in a group, compare your list with those of others.

2. What spiritual lessons have you learned from your study of 1 Corinthians thus far?

3. Henry Alford, *The Greek New Testament* (Chicago: Moody, 1958), 2:57.
4. Ibid.

Chart C

1 CORINTHIANS   PROBLEMS OF A LOCAL CHURCH

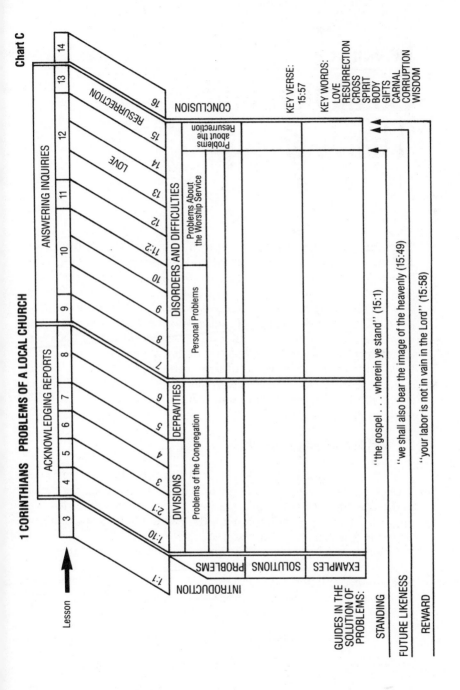

Lesson

3	4	5	6	7	8	9	10	11	12	13	14

ACKNOWLEDGING REPORTS   ANSWERING INQUIRIES

| 1:1 | 1:10 | 2:1 | 3 | 4 | 5 | 6 | 7 | 8 | 9 | 10 | 11:2 | 12 | 13 | 14 | 15 | 16 |

RESURRECTION

LOVE

INTRODUCTION

DIVISIONS | DEPRAVITIES | DISORDERS AND DIFFICULTIES | CONCLUSION

Problems of the Congregation | Personal Problems | Problems About the Worship Service | Problems about the Resurrection

GUIDES IN THE SOLUTION OF PROBLEMS: | PROBLEMS | SOLUTIONS | EXAMPLES

STANDING — "the gospel . . . wherein ye stand" (15:1)

FUTURE LIKENESS — "we shall also bear the image of the heavenly (15:49)

REWARD — "your labor is not in vain in the Lord" (15:58)

KEY VERSE: 15:57

KEY WORDS:
LOVE
RESURRECTION
CROSS
SPIRIT
BODY
GIFTS
CARNAL
CORRUPTION
WISDOM

21

Lesson 3

Salutation and Thanksgiving

Divine judgment originates from above, and that is the place where grace dwells also. So when Paul was moved by the Spirit to write this letter of exposure and condemnation of the various sins of God's people, he did not lose sight of the glorious truth of divine grace. Paul well knew that it was grace that brought the gospel to Corinth in the first place, and it was this same grace that was now able to revive the backslidden Corinthian believers. It should not surprise us, therefore, that the opening paragraphs of Paul's long letter make no mention of the problems of the local church but assure the readers that heaven has not disowned them. This is the bright and glorious introduction of the epistle we will be studying in this lesson.

I. PREPARATION FOR ANALYSIS

1. Sosthenes is not a main character in New Testament history, yet Paul chooses to recognize his brother in Christ by citing his name in the opening salutation of 1 Corinthians. Read Acts 18:17 for the reference to what may have been the same Sosthenes. Compare Acts 18:8 to learn his relationship to Crispus.

2. Keep in mind that Paul's last contacts with the Corinthians before writing this epistle were unpleasant ones (the "painful" visit and the severe letter noted in Lesson 1). If you were Paul sending the epistle, what would you write about in the first ten opening lines?

_____

_____

_____

II. ANALYSIS

Segment to be analyzed: 1:1-9
Paragraph divisions: at verses 1, 4, 9. Mark these divisions in your Bible.

A. General Analysis

1. Read the passage a few times, slowly and carefully. Underline key words and phrases as you read. How often does the phrase "Lord Jesus Christ" appear? On the following diagram record the immediate context of each appearance of that phrase.

"LAW OF CENTRALITY"

LORD
JESUS
CHRIST

What spiritual lessons are taught by this key phrase of 1 Corinthians?

_____

_____

_____

_____

2. Record your observations of the segment on an analytical chart similar to Chart D. (Words of the Bible text go inside the boxes; your own outlines, etc., go in the margins.)
3. Observe on the chart that most of the second paragraph is divided into three parts: past, present, future. Check the Bible text

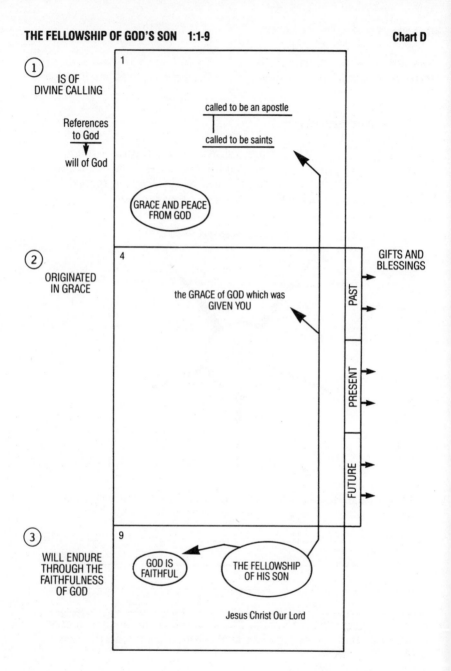

24

for this. (Note: The word "is" of verse 4 should read "was"; and "are" of verse 5 should read "were.")
Record on the chart the *gifts* and *blessings* associated with each time period.
4. Study all the references to God in the segment. Record this in the left-hand margin. Observe the attributes of God cited at the end of each paragraph.
5. Note the main topical study shove, with the master title *The Fellowship of God's Son.*
6. Record other topical studies as you continue your study in this rich portion of Scripture.

B. Paragraph Analysis

1. *Salutation*: 1:1-3
Complete the following parts of the salutation:

PERSON	DESCRIPTION
Paul	
and Sosthenes	
unto _____	

What does the phrase "both theirs and ours" (v.2) teach?

_____

_____

The combination "grace" and "peace" appears often in the Bible. What is meant by each word, and what is significant about the combination?

_____

_____

_____

Why do you think the order is "grace and peace" rather than "peace and grace"?

_____

2. *Thanksgiving*: 1:4-8
Observe in the King James Version that verses 4-8 are one sentence. Record this long sentence on Chart D, showing how each clause is related to the opening core, "I thank my God always on your behalf."[1] The common note is the word "you" in its various forms:

v. 4   "I thank my God always

    ON YOUR BEHALF,

      for the grace _____ ;

v. 5   that in every thing _____ ;

v. 6   even as _____ ;

v. 7   so that _____ ;

      _____ :

v. 8   who shall also _____ ,

      that ye may be _____ .

From your study of these verses, what were the various bases for Paul's thanksgiving to God for the Corinthian believers who were grieving him by their sins?

_____

_____

---

1. This exercise of recording the Bible text is called textual re-creation. For a detailed description of this phase of analysis, see Irving L. Jensen, *Independent Bible Study* (Chicago: Moody, 1963), pp. 126-33.

3. *The great affirmation*: 1:9
The very wording of this verse makes it stand out, as though to draw special attention to its grand truths. Compare this verse with 15:58 (the concluding verse of the main body of 1 Corinthians). How are they related?

_____

_____

How is each related to all the problems discussed in between the verses?

_____

_____

III. NOTES

1. *"Called to be an apostle of Jesus Christ through the will of God"* (1:1). Do you think the hardships of Paul's apostolic ministry were part of God's will? (Cf. 2 Cor. 11:23-31.)
2. *"Sanctified"* (1:2). The Greek word *hagiazo* has the prominent idea of *setting apart* for God's possession and use (John 17:17-19).
3. *"Grace"* (1:3). The Greek word is *charis*, which is the root of the word translated "gift." The word is found in every section of every epistle of Paul. Why is it such a key New Testament word?

_____

_____

In its classical Greek usage, the word originally referred to the realm of order and beauty.[2] Then it came to mean a desire on God's part to impart these good things to others. The New Testament extended the word to mean the *activity* to carry out that desire. So, in the words of Morgan, "Grace is ultimately the activity of God which puts at the disposal of sinning men and women all the things that give delight to Him."[3] Observe especially that grace is never *deserved* by man.
4. *"Ye come behind in no gift"* (1:7). God's gifts to the Corinthian believers were of three kinds: (1) salvation (cf. Rom. 5:15-17), (2) gifts in general, related to the whole life (cf. 1 Cor. 7:7), and (3)

2. See G. Campbell Morgan, *The Corinthian Letters of Paul*, p. 10.
3. Ibid.

27

special spiritual gifts (1 Cor. 12:1–14:40). Paul was probably referring to the last two kinds.

5. *"Confirm you unto the end"* (1:8). The word "confirm" intends
the ideas *assure, guarantee, give a foretaste of.* In Paul's day it was
a technical legal term for guaranteed securities.

IV. FOR THOUGHT AND DISCUSSION

1. Compare the phrases "will of God" (v. 1) and "grace of
God" (v.4). Do you believe that the will of God will never lead
you where the grace of God cannot keep you?

2. What is meant by the phrase "sanctified in Christ Jesus"
(1:2)? Consider these three kinds of sanctification: (1) positional
holiness, in Christ (Acts 20:32; 26:18; 1 Cor. 1:30), (2) progressive
spiritual maturing (Eph. 5:26; 2 Cor. 7:1), and (3) ultimate con-
forming to Christ's image (1 Thess. 5:23).

3. What do you like about the tone of Paul's opening to his
letter? What practical lessons can be learned from this?

4. Why is the *lordship* of Jesus Christ essential for Christian
living? Is it true that He is not Lord at all if He is not Lord of all?

5. How are you exercising your relation to Christ in terms of
fellowship? The word translated "fellowship" has the root word
common. (Cf. Acts 2:44.) As a believer, what do you have in common with Christ?

6. How would you describe a fellowship of saints living according to standards revealed in the Bible?

V. FURTHER STUDY

Extend your studies on the three important words *grace, sanctification*, and *fellowship.* For outside help, use an exhaustive concordance and a book on word study.[4]

VI. WORDS TO PONDER

The church of God which is at Corinth (1:2)

Reread this phrase by inserting the name and city of your
own local church. Then ponder the relationship of the local
church to the Body of Christ, the church universal. "The whole
teaching of the New Testament is that God has gained, and does

---

4. A recommended book on word study: W. E. Vine, *An Expository Dictionary of
New Testament Words.*

gain, something through His Church. It is a vehicle of vision, a medium of manifestation, a method by which He is able to do amongst men what, apart from that Church, He cannot do."[5]

5. Morgan, p. 12.

Lesson 4

Party Strife

Paul, in his forthright and honest manner, loses no time in telling the Corinthians why he is writing. Spiritual problems are dividing their fellowship, for one thing, and the apostle rebukes them sharply that these things ought not to be.

As you study this epistle chapter by chapter, you will want to analyze carefully the three main ingredients of each discourse.

1. *Identification of the problem.* Paul exposes the cancer of the Corinthians' sins, so that they will seek a cure. (Cf. Rom. 7:7, "I had not known sin, but by the law.")

2. *Solution for the problem.* No diagnosis without a prescription—this is Paul's pattern throughout the epistle as he counsels with the Corinthian patients concerning their spiritual maladies. He consistently refers them to the great Physician, assuring them of a divine cure if they will but obey the doctor's orders.

3. *Example of Paul.* Throughout the epistle Paul anticipates objections from the Corinthians that he is being too idealistic—for who (they would challenge) can have victory over such evils? Paul replies by sharing his own testimony of spiritual victories won in the power of Christ. These are some of the brightest and warmest portions of the letter.

I. PREPARATION FOR ANALYSIS

1. Observe on survey Chart C that 1:10–4:21 is one full section, called DIVISIONS (i.e., divisions in the church). The passage for this lesson is the first of four segments in that section. Scan the section paragraph by paragraph in your Bible, and record paragraph titles on Chart E. Do not spend too much time doing this, since you will be returning to the paragraphs in this and the following lessons. This is only for a general survey of Paul's treatment of the subject of divisions.

Lesson 4	Lesson 5	Lesson 6	Lesson 7

1:10 1:18 1:26 2:1 2:6 2:10 3:1 3:10 3:16 3:18 4:1 4:6 4:14 4:18 4:21

references to the problem

solutions

examples

As you complete each of Lessons 4-7, record your findings in the spaces provided at the bottom of the chart: references to the problem, solutions, examples.

2. Review the main thoughts of 1:1-9. Observe that Paul there does not even suggest that the Corinthians had some serious spiritual problems.

3. Recall the prominence of the phrase "Lord Jesus Christ" in 1:1-9. Note how 1:10 makes its appeal by that same name. What does this teach you about personal spiritual problems and their solutions?

_____

_____

4. What connection did each person mentioned in verses 12, 14, and 16 have to the church at Corinth? (Cephas is Peter; on Gaius, see *Notes*; on Stephanas, see 1 Cor. 16:15, 17.)

II. ANALYSIS

Segment to be analyzed: 1:10-31
Paragraph divisions: at verses 10, 18, 26. Mark these divisions in your Bible.

A. General Analysis

1. Read the passage, underlining key words and phrases as you read. Record these on Chart F.
2. Observe the main topical study on Chart F, with the title "The Word of the Cross." Make a brief study of this in the Bible text.
3. Observe on Chart F the three sets of topical studies:
Unity—Wisdom—Glory
Love—Faith—Humility
Common Believers—Saved Believers—Called Believers
Locate in each paragraph the various references to each part of these outlines. Make other topical studies on your own.

B. Paragraph Analysis

1. *Paragraph 1:10-17*
What two words in verses 10 and 11, respectively, identify the problem?

What forms of factionalism had developed, according to verse 12?

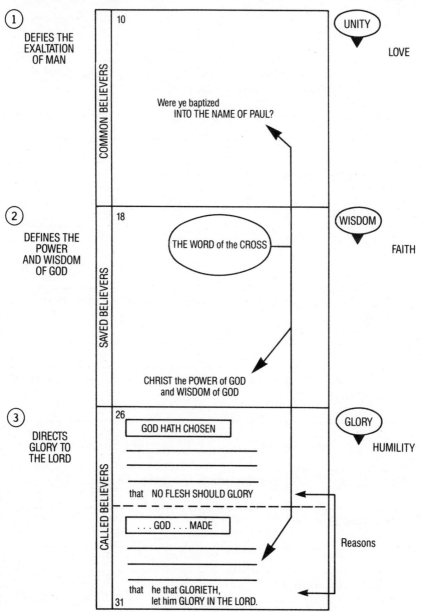

① DEFINES THE
EXALTATION
OF MAN

10

COMMON BELIEVERS

Were ye baptized
INTO THE NAME OF PAUL?

UNITY

LOVE

② DEFINES THE
POWER
AND WISDOM
OF GOD

18

SAVED BELIEVERS

THE WORD of the CROSS

CHRIST the POWER of GOD
and WISDOM of GOD

WISDOM

FAITH

③ DIRECTS
GLORY TO
THE LORD

26

CALLED BELIEVERS

GOD HATH CHOSEN

that   NO FLESH SHOULD GLORY

. . . GOD . . . MADE

that   he that GLORIETH,
31   let him GLORY IN THE LORD.

GLORY

HUMILITY

Reasons

Why would Paul condemn the group that claimed to be "of Christ" (v. 12)?

_____

_____

Compare the reading of this verse in *The Living Bible*. What does verse 10 say about solutions to the problem?

_____

_____

_____

What is a key repeated word in this verse?

_____

_____

Relate this to the word "fellowship" of 1:9.

_____

_____

What other words in verse 10 refer to the unity of believers in Christ?

_____

_____

In what ways do the examples of 1:13-17 speak to the problem of factionalism?

_____

_____

_____

What is the impact of each phrase: "Is Christ divided?" (1:13)

_____

"Was Paul crucified for you?" (1:13)

_____

_____

2. *Paragraph 1:18-25.*
How does the phrase "wisdom of words" of 1:17 lead into the main subject of this new paragraph?

_____

_____

Is this another spiritual problem of the Corinthian Christians, related to the problem of factionalism? If so, what solutions and examples are given?

_____

_____

Observe this repeated pattern in the paragraph:

verses 18-21		verses 22-25	
v. 18a	"For the preaching of the cross"	v. 23	"we preach Christ crucified
v. 18b	"but unto us which are saved"	v. 24	"but unto them which are called"
vv. 18b-21	"power of God" "wisdom of God"	vv. 24-25	"power of God" "wisdom of God"

Analyze the paragraph in view of the above structure. What does the paragraph teach about:
(a) the cross

_____

_____

(b) preaching the cross

_____

_____

(c) true wisdom

_____

_____

(d) divine power

_____

_____

(e) vanity of the human heart

_____

_____

What does this paragraph contribute to the solution of the problem of divisions in the church?

_____

_____

_____

3. *Paragraph 1:26-31*
What are the key repeated words and phrases here?

_____

_____

_____

Analyze the text around the two key phrases shown on Chart F: "God hath chosen" and "... God ... made." Observe how verses 29 and 31 conclude each of those teachings by showing the *reasons* for God's working this way. How do you think the Corinthians' exaltation of human wisdom was a cause for dissension among their ranks?

_____

_____

Record on Chart E what the three paragraphs of 1:10-31 contribute to Paul's discourse on divisions in the church.

III. Notes

1. *"I beseech you, brethren"* (1:10). The tenderness of Paul in dealing with the glaring sins of the Corinthian church is revealed by the opening word "beseech." The Greek word (*paracaleo*) means literally to call to one's side, and so suggests the ministry of an advocate. Morgan says the word "disannuls our loneliness and orphanage."[1]

2. *"I of Apollos"* (1:12). Among philosophically minded people such as the Corinthians, new schools of thought kept emerging, with one man championed as the founder and leader of each school. In Corinth this carried over into the Christian group, where cliques developed over distinctions between methods, emphases, and afflictions. (For example, Apollos may have been idolized because of his rhetorical style of preaching, while the credentials of Cephas [Peter] as one of the original twelve disciples may have been the key appeal to another "party.")

1. G. Campbell Morgan, *The Corinthian Letters of Paul*, p. 18.

3. *"Gaius"* (1:14). This may have been the Gaius of Romans 16:23, since Paul wrote Romans from Corinth.

4. *"Power"* (1:18). Two different words are translated "power' in this epistle. In this verse the word is *dunamis* (cf. "dynamite"), meaning "tremendous might"; the other word means "authority" (cf. 1 Cor. 9:12).

5. *"Jews require a sign"* (1:22). For examples of this, read Matthew 12:38; 16:1, 4; John 6:30.

6. *"Wisdom, and righteousness, and sanctification, and redemption"* (1:30). The Greek construction of the sentence sets off the word "wisdom" by itself. It appears that Paul intends the last three terms to illustrate and exemplify the first.[2] Study the three terms in the context of 1:30 in view of these comparisons:

"righteousness"	"sanctification"	"redemption"
past	present	future
positional	progressive	ultimate
Rom. 1:17	Rom. 6:19	Rom. 8:23

IV. FOR THOUGHT AND DISCUSSION

1. Have you ever been aware of cliques and "parties" in a local church? What is the root of such a problem? What can leaders and members of a local church do to help correct such a situation when it arises? How important is it to nip such things in the bud?

2. Study the context of "discord" in Proverbs 6:16-19.

3. What do you learn about the ordinance of water baptism from 1:13-17?

4. Philosophy (the word is from *filo*—love—and *sophia*—wisdom) is defined in the dictionary as the "study of the truth or principles underlying all knowledge." What is truth? (Cf. in 18:38.) What is the difference between knowledge and wisdom? What is the difference between the "wisdom of this world" (1:20) and the "wisdom of God" (1:24)?

5. What has this passage taught you about mental outlook and attitudes acceptable to God?

2. See Marvin R. Vincent, *Word Studies in the New Testament*, 3:194.

6. What is so natural and real and mandatory about the simple proclamation of the message of the cross?

V. FURTHER STUDY

Extend your study of the subject "truth" into the areas of divine revelation and human reason. Consider, for example, why the doctrine of eternal salvation must originate from divine revelation.

VI. WORDS TO PONDER

No one anywhere can ever brag in the presence of God (1:29, *The Living Bible*).

Lesson 5

1 Corinthians 2:1-16

The Mysteries of God Revealed

Paul continues discussing subjects introduced in 1:10-31; here his discourse is mainly a testimony. This testimony concerns his *word* ministry to the Corinthians on his first visit to the city. The clue to the testimonial nature of the chapter is the phrase "When I came to you" (2:1). As you study this chapter you will want to observe additional teachings about the subjects already introduced (e.g., God's wisdom), as well as teachings about new subjects. Bear in mind also that all of these are related to the central problem of divisions in the church, introduced in chapter 1.

I. PREPARATION FOR ANALYSIS

1. Read Isaiah 64:4, which Paul quotes freely in 1 Corinthians 2:9. Reconstruct the context of the Isaiah passage. Also, read Isaiah 40:13 and Romans 11:34 for background to 1 Corinthians 2:16a.
2. In this passage, as well as in 1:10-31, Paul emphasizes Christ's death but does not explicitly refer to His resurrection.[1] Try to account for the emphasis on crucifixion at this point.

II. ANALYSIS

Segment to be analyzed: 2:1-16
Paragraph divisions: at verses 1, 6, 10. Mark these divisions in your Bible.

---

1. Paul is not overlooking the doctrine of resurrection. It is interesting that it is this epistle that contains the classic New Testament passage on the resurrection body (chap. 15).

39

A. General Analysis

1. A clue that Paul is especially writing about his *word* ministry to the Corinthians is the repeated phrase "we speak." Underline in your Bible every occurrence of this and similar phrases in the segment.
2. Look for other key words and phrases in the segment. Record these on Chart G.
3. What are the pronouns of each of the paragraphs?

vv. 1-5 _____; vv. 6-9 _____; vv. 10-16 _____.
Which paragraphs are more doctrinal than testimonial?

_____

4. What is the main point of each paragraph?

_____

_____

_____

What would you say is a main theme of the segment?

_____

Compare your observations with those shown on Chart G. Observe especially this outline: Method, Message, Meaning. Read the segment again to see how the paragraphs are represented by this outline. Observe and record your own outlines of other subjects on the chart.

B. Paragraph Analysis

1. *The method of Paul's preaching*: 2:1-5
What do you learn here about Paul's methods and motives in preaching the gospel?

_____

_____

Note the references to the three Persons of the Trinity. What does Paul say here about his message?

_____

_____

2. *The message of Paul's preaching*: 2:6-9.
In what ways does Paul describe the message he preaches?

_____

40

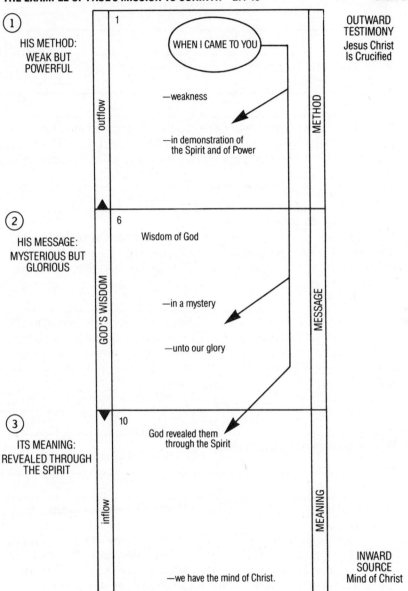

① HIS METHOD:
WEAK BUT
POWERFUL

② HIS MESSAGE:
MYSTERIOUS BUT
GLORIOUS

③ ITS MEANING:
REVEALED THROUGH
THE SPIRIT

1
outflow

WHEN I CAME TO YOU

—weakness

—in demonstration of
the Spirit and of Power

METHOD

6
GOD'S WISDOM

Wisdom of God

—in a mystery

—unto our glory

MESSAGE

10

God revealed them
through the Spirit

inflow

MEANING

—we have the mind of Christ.

16

OUTWARD
TESTIMONY
Jesus Christ
Is Crucified

INWARD
SOURCE
Mind of Christ

Could "wisdom of God" here mean the gospel of God? Circle in your Bible the first word "wisdom" in verse 7. What words in the remainder of the paragraph describe that "wisdom"?

_____

_____

What fruits and blessings come of this message?

_____

_____

The phrase "them that are perfect" is better translated "the mature," referring to spiritually mature believers. (Cf. 14:20; Heb 6:1-2.) What is the last description of believers made in the paragraph?

_____

_____

3. *Understanding God's wisdom*: 2:10-16
Read the first phrase of verse 10: "But God hath revealed them." The word "them" is supplied by the translator. It could read "it" (footnote in ASV*). If so, could "it" refer back to the word "wisdom" in verse 7?

_____

Observe how often the words "Spirit" and "know" appear in the paragraph. Use these as clues to the theme of the paragraph. Note the key word "revealed" in 2:10. Why must a mystery of God, a hidden wisdom, be revealed from heaven, if it is ever to be known?

_____

_____

Who is the agent of revelation?

_____

_____

On the Spirit's ministry of illumination to believers, read John 16:13-14.

There is an advance in Paul's theme from the first phrase, "God hath revealed" (2:10), to the last, "We have the mind of Christ" (2:16). Look for this progression as you record the meaning of each verse below. (Refer to a modern paraphrase for help in the meaning of some of the ambiguous phrases of this paragraph.) For example, use the following paraphrases:

*American Standard Version.

42

v. 13*b*—"interpreting spiritual truth to spiritual persons" (Berkeley)[2]

v. 15 —"But the spiritual man has insight into everything, and that bothers and baffles the man of the world, who can't understand him at all" (*The Living Bible*)

2:10 _____

2:11 _____

2:12 _____

2:13 _____

2:14 _____

2:15 _____

2:16 _____

After you have completed analyzing this segment, summarize your observations on Chart E of Lesson 4.

III. NOTES

1. *"A mystery"* (2:7). The word *mystery* appears twenty-seven times in the New Testament, most frequently in Paul's writings. It refers to God's hidden truth, known to man only through divine revelation. This is why human reason is incapable of discovering the truth.

2. *"Revealed"* (2:10). The Greek word is *apokalupto* (*apo*, "from"; and *kalupto*, "to cover"), meaning to remove the cover from, or unveil.

3. *"The natural man"* (2:14). The natural man is the unregenerate person in whom the Holy Spirit does not dwell (Rom. 8:9-11). "The Greek word rendered *natural* means 'dominated by the soul,' the principle of physical life."[3]

4. *"Judgeth all things"* (2:15). The word translated "judgeth" is the same word translated "discerned" in verse 14. The latter is the better translation for both verses.

5. *"We have the mind of Christ"* (2:16) The Greek word for "mind" is *nous*, meaning intellect or consciousness. Christians can *know* the mind of Christ, because they *have* the mind of Christ. "Incredible as it may sound, we who are spiritual have the very thoughts of Christ!" (2:16, Phillips).

2. Some expositors prefer this allowable rendering: "So we use the Holy Spirit's words to explain the Holy Spirit's facts" (*The Living Bible*).
3. Charles F. Pfeiffer and Everett F. Harrison, eds., *The Wycliffe Bible Commentary* (Chicago: Moody, 1962), p. 1233.

IV. FOR THOUGHT AND DISCUSSION

1. Do you think verse 2:2 refers to Paul's aim in (1) his preaching, (2) the Corinthian believers' living, or (3) both? In what ways can a Christian's life manifest to others only "Jesus Christ, and him crucified"?

2. What is wrong about preaching "with enticing words of man's wisdom" (2:4)? Evaluate the statement by one observer that "it is possible to sacrifice the prophet to the artist."

3. Was Paul anti-wisdom and anti-scholarship? Answer this in the light of 2:6-7. How do you think Paul would witness to a philosopher today who was searching for the truth about the universe? How would he deal with one who vainly boasted that the human mind was his god?

4. If an unsaved person is unable to discern the spiritual truths of the Spirit of God (2:14), how can he respond to the invitation of the gospel to be saved? What is the condition for salvation: faith or understanding? When a person is saved, does he know all there is to know of spiritual truth, or does he then begin to grow in knowledge? (Cf. 2 Pet. 3:18.)

5. Do you think 2:9 refers to heaven? Answer this in the light of 2:10*a*.

6. What practical spiritual lessons are taught in chapter 2 in addition to those related to the problems of partyism and sophisticated intellectualism?

V. FURTHER STUDY

Three subjects for extended study in the New Testament are (1) mystery, (2) wisdom, (3) the Holy Spirit's ministry of illumination and teaching. An exhaustive concordance and books on doctrine and word studies are the basic outside helps for such a study.

VI. WORDS TO PONDER

The Holy Spirit's power was in my words, proving to those who heard them that the message was from God (2:4*b*, *The Living Bible*).

Lesson 6

The Unity of God's Servants

After writing about his own service to God and the gospel's mysteries, Paul gets very personal and frank. In chapter 3 he writes about specific sins of which the Corinthian Christians were guilty. The apostle brings up again the underlying sin of divisions in the church and shows by various metaphors why the believers in Corinth should be working together in a spirit of unity. Paul's exclamation "We are labourers together with God" (3:9) is the core of his appeal in this passage.

In your study of chapter 3 you will be observing a large *variety* of content. Here are exposure, reproof, instruction, encouragement, and appeal—all in the compass of twenty-three relatively short verses. You should find this a very interesting chapter to analyze.

I. PREPARATION FOR ANALYSIS

1. Read 2 Timothy 3:16-17 for an identification of the various ministries of Scripture. As you study 1 Corinthians 3 observe how this inspired text functions in those ways.

2. Compare the first ten words of 2:1 with those of 3:1. What does this show as to Paul's continuity of thought from chapter 2 to chapter 3?

3. Review Chart E for what Paul has written thus far about the problem of divisions in the church.

II. ANALYSIS

Segment to be analyzed: 3:1-23
Paragraph divisions: at verses 1, 10, 16, 18[1]

1. Verse 9 could be considered a transitional verse between the first and second paragraphs, as will be shown later.

A. General Analysis

1. After you have marked the paragraph divisions in your Bible, read the segment paragraph by paragraph. Underline key words and phrases as you read.
2. How do the paragraphs differ as to their main points?

_____

_____

_____

_____

3. A key repeated phrase in the chapter is "ye are," followed by an identification. Locate these various references in the chapter. Compare your study with that shown on Chart H. What is Paul's purpose in instructing his readers as to whom they really are?

_____

4. What are the various metaphors used by Paul in the chapter?

_____

_____

_____

Compare this with Jesus' parabolic method.
5. In your own words, what is the main theme of the chapter?

_____

_____

_____

6. What is the climactic statement of the chapter?

_____

_____

7. As you proceed in your analysis, record various observations on Chart H. This will help you see the different parts in relation to the whole chapter.

B. Paragraph Analysis

1. *One field: 3:1-9*
Observe how the paragraph is divided:

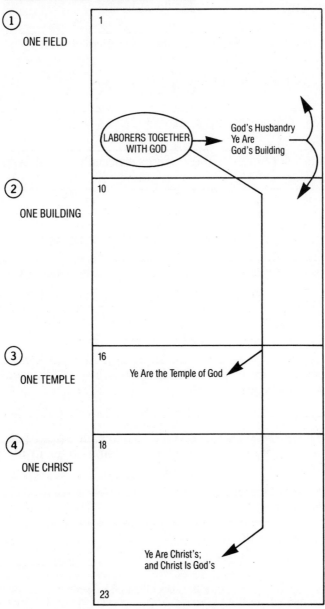

1 ONE FIELD

2 ONE BUILDING

3 ONE TEMPLE

4 ONE CHRIST

LABORERS TOGETHER WITH GOD

God's Husbandry
Ye Are
God's Building

Ye Are the Temple of God

Ye Are Christ's;
and Christ Is God's

3:1-2 —indictment of the readers, in a general way (key word:

_____

3:3 —identification of the specific sin:

_____

3:4 —description of the sin in the Corinthian church:

_____

3:5-9—proof of guilt and appeal for correction

_____

Who is the central person of verses 5-9?

_____

What different phrases of these verses especially appeal to you?

_____

_____

_____

What specific references to Christian _unity_ are made in verses 8 and 9?

_____

_____

How does the phrase "ye are God's husbandry [field, garden]" relate to what has gone before?

_____

How does the phrase "ye are God's building" refer to the next paragraph?[2]

_____

2. _One building: 3:10-15_
Identify each of the following, on the basis of the text:
the building (cf. v.9*b*):

_____

2. Mixed metaphors often appear but should not pose a problem in application. For example, 3:9 says that Christians are laborers in God's field, as well as being the field itself; and Christians are builders (3:10), as well as being the building itself (3:9).

48

owner of the building:

_____

the foundation:

_____

builder of the foundation:

_____

builder of the structure:

_____

building materials:

_____

test of the building:

_____

What is the relationship of Jesus Christ to God in this metaphor of
a building?

_____

How are believers related to each other, and to Christ and God?

_____

_____

_____

What other spiritual lessons are taught here besides those about
Christian unity?

_____

_____

_____

3. *One temple: 3:16-17*
The previous paragraph taught about a Christian's *works*—the out-
ward expression of his heart. This paragraph refers to his *worship*.
What words suggest this?

_____

_____

What are the main teachings of the two verses?

_____

_____

_____

How are they related to the underlying problem of divisions?

_____

_____

4. *One Christ: 3:18-23*
What is a key repeated word in verses 18-20?

_____

What contrasts do you see between the first three verses and the last three?

_____

_____

_____

What two things are compared in verse 21?

_____

_____

Analyze the list surrounded by the phrase "all ... are yours":
(a) Paul, or Apollos, or Cephas, or the world

_____

(b) life, or death

_____

(c) things present, or things to come

_____

What is Paul's point in this listing?

_____

_____

Observe the law of centrality in the diagram "Christ Is the Center." What is taught here about Christian unity?

_____

_____

III. NOTES

1. *"Carnal"* (3:1, 3). Two different words translated "carnal" are used in these verses. In verse 1, the idea is that of weakness, hence the associated word "babes" (v. 1). The Corinthian Christians should have been growing spiritually. In verse 3, the idea is that of willful sin, when one is mastered by that which is fleshly

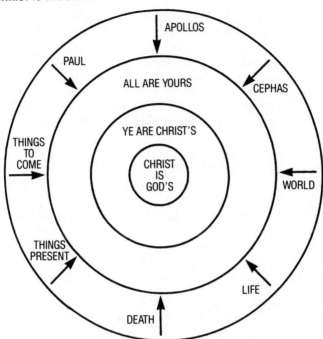

and material. "Weakness prolonged becomes willfulness. Refusal to respond to the milk of the Word prevents reception of the meat of the Word."[3]

2. *"Masterbuilder"* (3:10). This is the only place in the New Testament where this word appears. The Greek is *architekton*, from which our word *architect* is derived. The Phillips version is one of the few translations rendering the word as "architect." Paul laid the foundation (3:10) of the Corinthian church only in the sense that he was the servant used of God to lead the Corinthians to Christ and help them start a local church fellowship.

3. *"He shall suffer loss . . . as by [through] fire"* (3:15). This is a reference to loss of reward, not loss of salvation.

4. *"The temple of God"* (3:16). The Greek word translated "temple" is not *hieron*, referring to the large structure of Herod's Temple with all its precincts and courts, but *naos*, the inner shrine, the holy sanctuary.

---

3. Charles F. Pfeiffer and Everett F. Harrison, eds., *The Wycliffe Bible Commentary*, p. 1234.

IV. FOR THOUGHT AND DISCUSSION

1. How much positive doctrine and exhortation did you observe in this chapter? Why is it important to blend this with the negatives of reproof and correction when dealing with spiritual problems of an individual or group?

2. Christians are "labourers together with God" (3:9). What are ways in which Christians can blend their gifts and efforts with those of their brethren? In what ways do they work with God?

3. What are some of the differences between the following kinds of persons:

(a) the natural man (2:14)
(b) the carnal "babes" (3:1)
(c) the carnal-willful man (3:3)
(d) the spiritual man (2:15)

4. What does this chapter teach about the place of leaders and followers in the work of the church?

5. Paul says that all believers should labor *together* in God's vineyard. Is each believer accountable for *his own* works? What does Paul say about this in chapter 3?

V. FURTHER STUDY

Inquire further into what the New Testament teaches about future judgment of believers, at the judgment seat of Christ (see Rom. 14:10; 2 Cor. 5:10).

VI. WORDS TO PONDER

Where there is jealousy and party-strife among you, are you not living by earthly standards, behaving like unregenerate men? (3:3, *An Expanded Paraphrase,* by F. F. Bruce)

Lesson 7

Paul's Defense of His Ministry

Paul was aware that many of the Corinthian church's problems were related to him and his ministry. He had already referred in his epistle to the divisive party spirit ("I of Paul," "I of Apollos," etc.). But there were also those in the church who were openly judging and criticizing him and who were questioning the honesty of his intentions. So in chapter 4 Paul writes what might be called a defense of his ministry.[1] He would have been the first to say that the ministry of the gospel stands on its own merits, without need for defense. But the situation at Corinth forced him to clarify the issues for the good of the local church as a whole. Hence this chapter.

I. PREPARATION FOR STUDY

Paul's tone and approach varies from paragraph to paragraph in this chapter. For example, it is important that you read verses 8 and 10 as irony, or you will miss Paul's point. This tone is not made clear in the King James Version. Read the verses first in that version, and compare them with the following paraphrases of *The Living Bible*.[2]

> You seem to think you already have all the spiritual food you need. You are full and spiritually contented, rich kings on your thrones, leaving us far behind! I wish you really were already on your thrones, for when that time comes you can be sure that we will be there, too, reigning with you (4:8).

---

1. In 2 Corinthians 10-13 Paul writes an extended defense of his ministry.
2. The Berkeley Version presents v. 8 in a series of questions, still retaining the tone of satire.

Religion has made us foolish, you say, but of course you are all such wise and sensible Christians! We are weak, but not you! You are well thought of, while we are laughed at (4:10).

It would be profitable for you, before beginning to analyze the text of the King James Version, to read the entire chapter in one or two modern versions. After you have done that, identify the tone of each of the paragraphs:

4:1-5

4:6-13

4:14-17

4:18-21

(Compare your conclusions with those shown on Chart I.)

II. ANALYSIS

Segment to be analyzed: 4:1-21
Paragraph divisions: at verses 1, 6, 14, 18

A. General Analysis

1. Read the chapter once or twice in your study version, underlining key words and phrases.
2. What is the main subject of each paragraph? (Compare Chart I.)

---

3. Record on Chart I other observations you have made concerning the content of each paragraph.

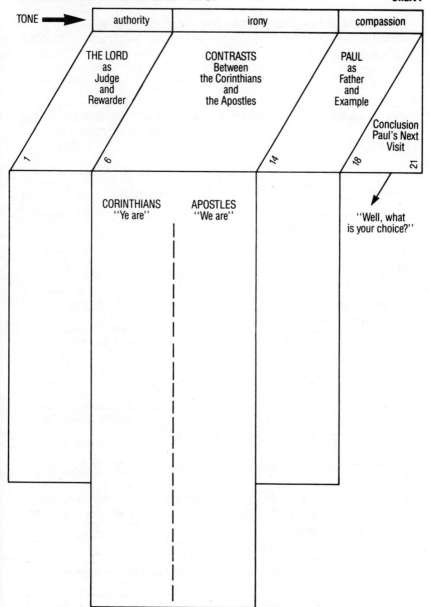

TONE ➡

| authority | irony | compassion |

THE LORD
as
Judge
and
Rewarder

CONTRASTS
Between
the Corinthians
and
the Apostles

PAUL
as
Father
and
Example

Conclusion
Paul's Next
Visit

1   6   14   18   21

CORINTHIANS
"Ye are"

APOSTLES
"We are"

"Well, what
is your choice?"

55

B. Paragraph Analysis

1. *The Lord as judge and rewarder: 4:1-5*
What two words does Paul use to identify his work, and what does each mean? (4:1)

_____

_____

Read 4:4*a* thus: "My conscience is clear, but even that isn't final proof" (*The Living Bible*). What does this paragraph teach about:
(a) What is required in Christian work:

_____

(b) judges that are not dependable:

_____

(c) the ultimate judge:

_____

(d) the time of judgment:

_____

(e) the consequences of judgment:

_____

2. *Contrasts between the Corinthians and the apostles: 4:6-13*
What evil does Paul condemn in verses 6 and 7?

_____

_____

How is this a clue to the intention of the ironical statement of verse 8 (given above in paraphrase form)?

_____

_____

Record on Chart I, in the appropriate columns, every description of the Corinthians and of the apostles. What does this teach you about the following:
(a) *The falsehood of conceit*

_____

_____

(b) *The trials of faithfulness*

_____

_____

Compare the time reference *"now* ye are" (4:8) with "judge nothing *before the time"* (4:5). What does this suggest concerning the
Corinthians?

_____

_____

_____

Compare the last phrase of this paragraph with the last phrase of
the first paragraph.

_____

_____

3. *Paul as father and example: 4:14-17*
What is Paul's tone here?

_____

_____

What is the key command of the paragraph?

_____

_____

What is the command based on (v.15)?

_____

_____

Is Paul conceited in the things he writes here? Justify your answer.

_____

_____

4. *Conclusion to the section: 4:18-21*
How is this paragraph a conclusion to section 1:10–4:21?

_____

_____

Relate verse 20 to verse 8.

_____

_____

How does the verse relate to all that Paul has written in 1:10–4:21?

_____

57

What are the three references to "come"?
v. 18

___

v. 19

___

v. 21

___

What options does Paul leave with the Corinthian church? (4:21)

___

How would the manner of his next visit depend on their reaction to this epistle?

___

III. NOTES

1. *"Ministers"* (4:1). The word translated "ministers" is different from that of 3:5. Here the word means literally an "under-rower," that is, one who in New Testament times rowed in the lower tier of oars on a large ship. Thus it denoted any subordinate acting under another's direction. The word in this context focuses attention on Christ, whom Paul had just exalted in the climactic verse of 3:23.

2. *"Stewards"* (4:1). In Paul's day a man who had the responsibility of overseeing the estate of a landowner was called a steward. He was put in charge of the estate. (Cf. Luke 16:1.) This is the background of the transaction of 4:1*b*, "who have been put in charge of God's secret truths" (TEV*).

3. *"Not to think of men above that which is written"* (4:6). Observe by the italics in your King James Version that the words "of men" are not in the original text. The Berkeley Version renders the phrase as "not to go beyond what is written," with the footnote that "everything is to be weighed by what God has revealed in His Word."

4. *"Appointed to death ... made a spectacle unto the world"* (4:9). Paul's language fits either of these two scenes:

> They were doomed to death, like condemned criminals, or
> prisoners, who fought with wild beasts and seldom survived at

Today's English Version.

58

the close of pagan festivals and exhibitions. Or, Paul may have had in mind the triumphal procession of a Roman general, at the end of which walked those captured soldiers who were being taken to the arena to fight with wild beasts.[3]

IV. FOR THOUGHT AND DISCUSSION

1. What do you consider to be important qualities of service to Christ? Why does Paul single out *faithfulness*? (4:2; cf. Matt 25:21-23).
2. Should Christians think about future rewards in heaven while they work for Christ on earth? Justify your answer.
3. What undergirds a Christian while he experiences severe trials in his labors for the gospel?
4. Paul writes about "my ways which be in Christ" (4:17). Is your life seen by others as a walk *in Christ*?
5. Think about Paul's statement "I will come to you shortly, if the Lord will" (4:19). What does this reveal about Paul, the Lord, and the relationship between the two?
6. Visualize the members of the Corinthian church hearing an elder reading Paul's questions of verse 21 for the first time. What do you think were some of their inner responses?

V. A SUMMARY EXERCISE

Complete your entries on Chart E, with which you have been working in these past few lessons. Think over the different ways Paul has approached the basic problem of divisions in the church. What is your estimate of Paul's perception of human nature?

VI. WORDS TO PONDER

Now the most important thing about a servant is that he does just what his master tells him to (4:2, *The Living Bible*).

---

3. Charles F. Pfeiffer and Everett F. Harrison, eds., *The Wycliffe Bible Commentary*, p. 1236.

Three Alarming Evils in the Church

Paul now focuses on other kinds of evil practiced by the Corinthians and that had been reported to him. The severity of his reproof (e.g., "I speak to your shame," 6:5) is an indication of the awfulness of these spiritual cancers plaguing the church he had founded.

The three main problems discussed in this passage are:
1. Licentiousness (5:1-13)
2. Lawsuits (6:1-11)
3. Libertinism (6:12-20)

We should remind ourselves again that the problems of this ancient church are not foreign to the churches of the twentieth century. The sinful nature of man is changeless.

I. PREPARATION FOR ANALYSIS

1. Decide now how much of this lesson you want to study in one unit. It is recommended that the lesson be divided into three study units, one unit per problem as listed above.

2. In your study thus far you have seen that Paul's treatment of the problems in the Corinthian church takes on various forms. As you study this lesson observe various combinations of diagnostic, remedial, punitive, and preventive counsel.

3. With the help of a concordance or a word-study book, observe how frequently the New Testament refers to the sin of fornication.[1] Also read Genesis 35:22; 49:4; Deuteronomy 22:22, 30; 27:20; Leviticus 18:8; 1 Chronicles 5:1; 2 Samuel 16:22; and Amos 2:7 for background to 1 Corinthians 5:1.

---

1. The New Testament word "fornication" generally refers to any kind of sin against the seventh commandment, "Thou shalt not commit adultery." It is illicit sexual union of any kind.

4. Two sacred festivals in the first month (Nisan) of the Jewish sacred year are the Feast of the Passover followed immediately by the week-long Feast of Unleavened Bread. Read Exodus 12:1-15 and Deuteronomy 16:1-8 concerning the origins and purposes of these feasts. When viewed as types of New Testament truths, the Passover typifies Christ as the atonement for our sins, and partaking of unleavened bread typifies the sanctifying and cleansing work of the Holy Spirit in the life of a person, once he has been saved. Keep these typical truths in mind as you study 5:6-8. (A subject for further study in this connection could be the New Testament passages that assign these types to the two feasts.)

II. ANALYSIS

Segments to be analyzed: 5:1-13; 6:1-11; 6:12-20
Paragraph divisions: at verses 5:1, 6, 9; 6:1, 9, 12, 15, 18

As you study each of the three segments of this section, observe all that is said about (1) the evil, (2) the correction, and (3) the doctrine.

A. Segment 5:1-13:   Licentious Living

Recall from your study of Lesson 1 how depraved the moral condition of Corinth was. Then imagine how shocking it must have been to Paul to learn that someone in the church was guilty of a sin not even acceptable to many unsaved in Corinth.

1. *The evil*
Actually, two sins are cited. What are they?
v. 1

_____

v. 2

_____

In view of the remainder of the chapter, which of the two sins disturbed Paul more—the sin of the church as a whole or the sin of the individual fornicator? Why?

_____

_____

2. *The correction*
Paul had different things to say about how to deal with the particular sins and with the loose attitude that generated them.

61

(a) *Attitude*. The Corinthian church's attitude was this:

_____ (5:2*a*, 6*a*), whereas it should have been

this:_____ (5:2).

(b) *Action*. What verses in the chapter give instruction as to what a church should do in cases like this?

_____

_____

_____

What procedure for expulsion is described in 5:4-5? ("When ye are gathered together, and my spirit" may be read, "You must hold a meeting at which I shall be with you in spirit"[2]). How can members and leaders of a church see to it that action by the congregation is taken only (1) "in the name of our Lord Jesus Christ" and (2) "with the power of our Lord Jesus Christ"?

_____

_____

_____

Most expositors agree that 5:5*a* is difficult to interpret precisely. What do you think is meant by the verse? Compare such passages as 1 Timothy 1:20; 1 John 5:16-19; 1 Corinthians 11:30; Acts 5:1-11.

_____

_____

_____

(c) *Avoidance*. Verse 9 is a key to the prevention of acts of fornication: "Stop associating with sexually immoral people" (Williams). Reflect on this.

Observe that verse 9 does not identify the fornicators as either unsaved persons or professing Christians. What does Paul say in 5:10-13 about (1) the desirable relationship between a believer and an unsaved immoral person

_____

_____

(2) the desirable relationship between a moral Christian and an immoral professing Christian?

_____

_____

2. F. F. Bruce, *The Letters of Paul: An Expanded Paraphrase.*

For an interesting paraphrase of 5:9-13, with a different interpretation of "But now" (5: 11), read *The Living Bible* or *Today's
English Version*.

3. *The doctrine*

Read chapter 5 once again, noting its few brief doctrinal statements (e.g., "that the spirit may be saved in the day of the Lord Jesus," 5:5). If you are studying in a group, discuss each one. A
prominent doctrine is the last statement of verse 7: "For even
Christ our passover is sacrificed for us." At first glance the statement seems out of place, without any connection with the first
part of verse 7. To see the connection, recall the time sequence of
the Feast of the Passover and the Feast of Unleavened Bread, and
their typical significance. Keep in mind what was studied earlier in
this lesson about these two feasts, and on that basis justify the following reading of 5:7-8:

> Sweep out the old leaven, in order to become, so to speak,
> a fresh mass of dough, as free from leaven in fact as you are holy
> in God's sight. I am using this language because our passover
> sacrifice has already been offered up—our passover sacrifice, of
> course, is Christ. Therefore let us celebrate our festival of unlea-
> vened bread, having got rid of our old leaven.[3]

Paul's point here centers on the time references, thus:

(a) Christ our passover *has already been* sacrificed (our
atonement).

(b) *Now* therefore, let us live like Christians (our sanctification).

B. Segment 6:11: Lawsuits in the Public Courts

Paul here is not writing off the place of the public courts. His
plea to the Christian community is that they settle differences
among themselves, without going to the courts about them. Before studying this passage, refer to the *Notes* for an alternate possible rendering of 6:4.

1. *The evil*

What strong words in 6:1-8 does Paul use to indict the Corinthian
Christians guilty of this evil practice?

_____

_____

3. Ibid.

How does Paul describe the public courts?

_____

Do you see any suggestion here of a court system that was corrupt? Or is Paul merely recognizing that a pagan judge cannot decide in a case involving Christians since he does not have a perspective from within the kingdom of God (cf.2:8)? Does Paul write in these verses about the offense that brings on a suit in the first place? Compare this with the problem discussed in 5:1-13.

_____

_____

2. *The correction*
Record what each of the following verses says about *what should be*:
6:1

_____

6:4 (see *Notes*)

_____

6:7*b*

_____

Record what each of the following verses says about the *bases* for Christians staying out of the public courts:
6:2

_____

6:3

_____

6:5

_____

What is your reaction to Paul's plea of 6:7*b*?

_____

How can such passive submission repair and restore relationships between people? (Cf. Luke 6:29ff.)

_____

_____

3. *The doctrine*

The doctrinal passages in 1 Corinthians, whether they be short or long, are the refreshing oases. Spend much of your time studying these. What doctrines are taught in 6:2-3? (For 6:2, cf. John 5:22; Matt. 19:28; Luke 22:28ff.; Rev. 3:21; for 6:3, cf. Jude 6 and 2 Pet. 2:4.)

_____

_____

The major block of doctrine in this passage is 6:9-11. Analyze it carefully to determine these:

(a) What does it teach?

(b) Why is it located in the context of the problems of lawsuits and libertinism? (See diagram for a suggestion.)

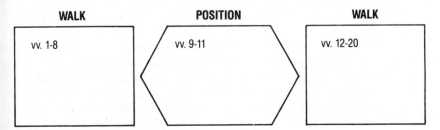

WALK	POSITION	WALK
vv. 1-8	vv. 9-11	vv. 12-20

The structure of this interesting paragraph will help you answer the above questions. Complete this:

"Know ye not that

the UNRIGHTEOUS shall not inherit _____ ?

_____

_____

_____

And | SUCH WERE | some of you:

But | YE ARE | washed,

　　ye are_____

　　ye are_____

　　　　　　in the _____

　　　　　　and by the _____ ."

C. Segment 6:12-20: Libertine Attitude Concerning Fornication

Paul does not cite in these verses any specific instance of evils committed by the Corinthians.[4] But the style and tone of the entire segment clearly indicate he is referring to existing abuses.

1. *The evil*

Various things should be observed in this segment to identify the evils Paul is diagnosing. Read the passage to discover its main emphasis. What is the key word repeated frequently?

_____

Underline its every appearance in the text. Note the two references to fornication. It is interesting to observe that this word appears in connection with all three problems of the section 5:1–6:20. (Locate all the references.)

_____

An unrepentant sinner will usually try to excuse or justify his sin. It appears that at least some of the Corinthians who were guilty of fornication maintained that their liberty in Christ allowed them unrestricted expression in all areas of life, if that gave them pleasure. Beginning with the true statement that "food is for the stomach, and the stomach is for food" (6:13, TEV), they concluded that therefore the body is for fornication and fornication is for the body. What was Paul's clear reaction to that (6:13*b*)?

_____

_____

_____

What things does Paul say in this segment about the sin of fornication?

_____

_____

_____

2. *The correction and the doctrine*

Because doctrinal statements in this passage are closely interwoven in the pattern of correction, we will study both at the same time. It is interesting to observe that the Corinthians were acquainted with many of the doctrines that Paul was teaching here,

4. Bruce's *Expanded Paraphrase* makes a specific reference in the opening verse: "'all things are permissible for me,' you say—yes, but not all things are profitable."

as indicated by the repetition of "Know ye not" throughout chapters 5 and 6.

(a) *Correction of a libertine attitude.* What is the difference between liberty and license?

_____

_____

(b) What is implied in the first phrase of 6:12?[5]

_____

_____

Compare 10:23 in the context of the subject of eating meat that had been offered in sacrifice to idols. Study the first antithetical statements of 6:12-13. Observe the common word "but." What Christian attitude is Paul appealing to in connection with "permissible" things?

_____

_____

(b) *Counsel on how to be victor over the temptation of fornication.* Fornication is a sin of the body. In fact, writes Paul, "he that committeth fornication sinneth *against his own body*" (6:18). So Paul teaches a host of truths about the body to help Christians gain victory over the temptation of fornication. Read 6:12-20 again, and make a list of eight to ten truths and commands about the body which, if believed and put to practice, would be of help to the tempted Christian. (For example, don't overlook the obvious command "flee fornication," v. 18*a*.)

v. 13

_____

_____

v. 14

_____

_____

v. 15

_____

_____

5. *The Living Bible* reads, "I can do anything I want to if Christ has not said 'No.'" Its footnote reads, "Obviously Paul is not here permitting sins such as have just been expressly prohibited in verses 8 and 9. He is talking about indifferent matters such as eating meat offered to idols."

v. 16

_____

_____

v. 17

_____

_____

v. 18

_____

_____

v. 19

_____

_____

v.20

_____

_____

III. NOTES

1. *"Ye ... have not rather mourned"* (5:2). The Corinthians "found it hard to hate the sensuality which in their earlier days they had regarded as divine."[6]

2. *"Deliver such an one unto Satan for the destruction of the flesh"* (5:5). (Cf. 1 Tim. 1:20.) The Berkeley Version footnote says that the word rendered "destruction" "does not of necessity carry the thought of annihilation but rather defilement or ruin.... The believer who continues to sin, such as the man described in this passage, may be given over to Satan so that he may be brought under conviction of sin and turned back to the place of obedience to God." Any interpretation of this verse, difficult as the verse is, must recognize that (1) deliverance to Satan is only by the permissive will of God (cf. 5:4), and (2) the destruction is of the person's "flesh," that is, the "carnal side of his personality."[7]

3. *"A little leaven"* (5:6). This leaven, a symbol of evil could refer to the instance of incest (5 :1) or to the vain glorying of 5:6a.

4. *"Put away from among yourselves"* (5:13). The appeal is clearly purity of testimony, with no compromise in the church. "In

6. L. Pullan, quoted by Leon Mobs, *The First Epistle of Paul to the Corinthians*, p. 25.
7. See G. Campbell Morgan, *The Corinthian Letters of Paul*, p. 58.

Israel God required capital punishment of gross sinners, so that the demand for banishment from the church under the new dispensation does not amaze us."[8]

5. *"Set them to judge"* (6:4). This verse may also be translated as a question: "When, however, you do have an everyday case, do you appoint for judges those in the church who have no standing?" (Berkeley).

6. *"All things are lawful"* (6:12). The word translated "lawful" means "permitted" (cf. John 5:10; 2 Cor. 12:4). The word comes from the same root as "power," so that a play on words is detected in Paul's testimony of 6:12*b*: "All things are in my power, but I will not be brought under the power of anything."

7. *"Flee fornication"* (6:18). The Greek tense calls for the reading "Make it your habit to flee."

8. *"Sinneth against his own body"* (6:18). Morris compares fornication with other sins of the body:

> Other sins will occur to us which have their effects on the body. But this sin, and this sin only, means that a man takes that body which is "a member of Christ" and puts it into a union which "blasts his own body" (Way). Other sins against the body, e.g. drunkenness or gluttony, involve the use of that which comes from without the body. The sexual appetite rises from within. They serve other purposes, e.g. conviviality. This has no other purpose than the gratification of the lusts. They are sinful in the excess. This is sinful in itself.[9]

9. *"Ye are bought with a price"* (6:20). The price was the blood of Christ (Acts 20:28; 1 Pet. 1: 18-21). "The figure is that of sacral manumission, whereby a slave, by paying the price of his freedom into the temple treasury, was regarded thereafter as the slave of the god and no longer the slave of his earthly master."[10]

IV. FOR THOUGHT AND DISCUSSION

1. How can one sin in a congregation affect the whole group (5:6)? Can you think of illustrations of this in Bible history? How are sincerity and truth (5:8) guardians of a pure church? "The history of the Church shows that the Church pure is the Church pow-

---

8. F. W. Grosheide, *Commentary on The First Epistle to the Corinthians*, p. 131.
9. Morris, pp. 102-3.
10. Charles F. Pfeiffer and Everett F. Harrison, eds., *The Wycliffe Bible Commentary*, p. 1239.

erful; and the Church patronized and tolerant towards evil is the Church puerile and paralyzed."[11]

2. What should be a Christian's relationship to an unsaved person and to a believer out of fellowship with Christ? Consider such situations as: friend, partner, associate, engaged couple, mate, neighbor.

3. What are your views on Christian liberty in such areas as dress, entertainment, activities on the Lord's Day, and so forth? Evaluate this comment: "Paul acknowledges Christian liberty but makes clear that the question whether or not to use it in a certain case does not depend on the liberty itself but on the circumstances outside of it (see I Cor. 8:9; cf. also Gal. 5:13; I Pet. 2:16)."[12]

4. Why is church discipline so important? Are churches generally lax in this area today? What attitudes in the church board or congregational meeting can mar the worthy intentions of such severe discipline?

5. Granted that the Christian must make it his habit to flee the very thought of sexual sin such as fornication, how can he develop and maintain this necessary habit? Think of different Bible verses that will supply some answers here.

6. Now that you have got a more intimate glimpse of the constituency of the church at Corinth, does it surprise you that Paul addressed this letter "to them that are *sanctified* in Christ Jesus, called to be *saints*" (1:2)?

V. FURTHER STUDY

The subjects of church discipline and evil associations are recommended for further study in the New Testament.

VI. WORDS TO PONDER

God has bought you with a great price. So use every part of your body to give glory back to God, because He owns it (6:20, *The Living Bible*).

11. Morgan, p. 57.
12. Grosheide, p. 144.

70

To Marry or Not to Marry

Paul begins answering questions that the Corinthians had directed to him via messengers and letters. Chart J shows this main divisional point, at 7:1.

CONTEXT OF CHAPTER 7   **Chart J**

	1:10 ACKNOWLEDGING REPORTS		7:1 ANSWERING INQUIRIES		15:58	
INTRODUCTION	Problems of the Congregation		Personal Problems	11:2 Problems About the Worship Service	15:1 Problems About the Resurrection	CONCLUSION
	DIVISIONS	5:1 DEPRAVITIES	DISORDERS AND DIFFICULTIES			

It is interesting to observe that Paul devoted the first part of his epistle to subjects about which the Corinthians had not written, leaving the last part of the letter to answer their inquiries. Can you think of some good reasons for Paul's writing his letter this way?

The subject of chapter 7 is that of marriage and personal problems that the Corinthians encountered relating to it. It should be kept in mind that the very fact of an inquiry suggests *existing* problems as well as *anticipated* problems.

I. PREPARATION OR ANALYSIS

1. False conclusions are easily made from chapter 7 if the local Corinthian situation and the larger context of Paul's epistles are not recognized. Let us look at these briefly:

(a) *Local Corinthian situation.* We do not know exactly how the Corinthians' questions were worded. If we did, some of the difficult aspects of chapter 7 would disappear. For example, the Corinthians' former heathen exaltation of celibacy could have prompted them to ask Paul if celibacy for Christians was not the state that all Christians should cherish. Paul's reply was, " [True,] it is good for a man not to touch a woman; *nevertheless*, let each man have his own wife, and let each woman have her own husband, because [if this normal pattern for the human race is broken], fornication [is inevitable]" (7:1).

Another local situation about which we can only speculate is the kind and extent of "distress" (7:26) that was threatening the Corinthian Christians at this time. It could well have been severe persecution, in which case Paul's counsel to the Corinthians was to postpone marriage for the time being (e.g., 7:26-27).

In studying chapter 7 it must also be remembered that sexual immorality ("fornication") was an evil threatening the survival of the Corinthian church. This problem must have had much to do with how Paul answered the questions about marriage.

(b) *Paul's full teaching on marriage.*[1] A reading of all of Paul's letters reveals that the apostle commended marriage as a high and holy estate. Read, for example, Ephesians 5:22-23. In 1 Timothy 4:3 Paul speaks of "forbidding to marry" as a doctrine of demons (4:1). In 1 Corinthians 7:12-16 Paul discusses the problems of mixed marriages with unbelievers. In 2 Corinthians 6:14 his advice is that the unmarried Christian can avoid such problems by not marrying an unbeliever. Many other references outside of 1 Corinthians could be cited here.

2. Chapter 7 contains some unusual statements about the origins of Paul's advice (e.g., "To the rest speak I, not the Lord," 7:12). Record these below:

7:6

---

1. G. Campbell Morgan correctly observes that no attempt is made in 1 Corinthians to state the Christian doctrine of marriage in its fullness (*The Corinthian Letters of Paul*, p. 85).

7:10

___

7:12

___

7:25

___

7:40

___

Three important things should be recognized here:

(a) Such a phrase as "I have no commandment of the Lord" (7:25) means that Paul had no express command of Jesus, written or oral, that he could quote on the subject. (For example, he could quote Matt. 19:6 for his counsel of 7:10.)

(b) Paul made clear that even his own "judgment" (opinion) (7:25, 40) was of divine direction (read 7.40).

(c) The chapter deals with actions permitted as well as actions commanded. In both situations the authority of Paul's counsel (recognized by us now as Scripture but to the Corinthians then as a personal letter) was of divine origin.

II. ANALYSIS

Segment to be analyzed: 7:1-40
Paragraph divisions: at verses 1, 8, 12, 17, 25, 32, 36, 39

A. General Analysis

Use the analytical Chart K as a work sheet to record your observations as you analyze the text. Read the chapter through once, observing the following:

1. The first two paragraphs are similar to the last two. In what ways? (Compare your answer with Chart K.)

2. The middle four paragraphs are of two pairs, as shown on the chart. Read the paragraphs again to see this pattern.

3. Observe how the first two verses of the first paragraph are restated, in a different way, in the first two verses of the second paragraph. Watch for other kinds of repetitions in the chapter.

B. Paragraph Analysis

As you analyze the text more minutely, identify or derive the following three things in each paragraph. (This triad is the core of all Bible study.)

1	1 celibacy is good
	2 marriage is normal
8	3 indissolubility of marriage
12	SITUATION: UNEQUAL YOKE
OBEDIENCE TO THE LORD'S CALLING — **17**	
25	SITUATION: DISTRESS (PERSECUTION?)
DEVOTION AND SERVICE TO THE LORD — **32**	
36	1 marriage is good
	2 celibacy is better (in certain circumstances)
39	3 indissolubility of marriage
40	

(a) the Corinthian color (local situation)
(b) the universal, timeless principles
(c) present-day applications
Selected questions and directions are given below to help you in your analysis of each paragraph. Extend your study beyond these suggestions.

1. *Paragraph 7:1-7.*
What value does Paul place on celibacy?

_____

On marriage?

_____

How is the word "render" a key to the marital obligations cited in verses 3-5?

_____

_____

How is verse 7*b* the key to the main question, to marry or not to marry?

_____

_____

Account for Paul's wish in verse 7*a*.

_____

_____

2. *Paragraph 7:8-11.*
What teachings does this paragraph add to those already discussed in the chapter?

_____

_____

3. *Paragraph 7:12-16.*
In verse 8 Paul addresses the unmarried parties; in verse 9, the married. Now, beginning at verse 12, he addresses "the rest," which here means married couples where one mate is an unbeliever. Why may there have been many mixed marriages (7:12-13) in the Corinthian church at this time?

_____

What do you think is meant by "sanctified" in verse 14?

_____

Is it synonymous with salvation? (Cf. 1 Tim. 4:5.)

_____

What thought is antecedent to each of the following:
(a) "but God hath called us to peace" (7:15)

_____

(b) "for what knowest thou [etc.]" (7:16)

_____

Refer to various modern versions for different views on Paul's intentions here.
4. *Paragraph 7:17-24: Obedience to the Lord's calling.*
This is the key doctrinal passage of the chapter. Spend much time analyzing it. What is the key repeated word?

_____

Compare this with the phrase "proper gift" in 7:7. List the various truths about "calling" taught here.

_____

_____

How does this paragraph answer the question, to marry or not to marry?

_____

_____

Is the answer made clear?
5. *Paragraph 7:25-31.*
As indicated earlier, the local situation at this time was one of great distress (7:26). What words and phrases in the paragraph suggest this?

_____

_____

_____

Note all the references to *time* in the paragraph, whether stated or implied. Observe in the *Living Bible* paraphrase how this time element is emphasized.

What is the point of 7:29-31?

How does this paragraph answer the question, to marry or not to marry?

6. *Paragraph 7:32-35: Devotion and service to the Lord.*
Note the repetition of "the Lord" in these verses. What is the context in each case?

Observe the opening and closing phrases: "without carefulness [anxiety]" and "without distraction." Is Paul here trying to shame the one who chooses to marry? (Cf. 7:35.)

Is Paul correct in what he says about the divided cares of a Christian husband or wife?

Does the following modern paraphrase represent Paul's purpose in writing 7:32-35 (note the word "ideal"):

> I tell you these things to help you; I am not putting difficulties in your path but setting before you an ideal, so that your service of God may be as far as possible free from worldly distractions (7:35, Phillips).

7. *Paragraph 7:36-38.*
Two differing schools of thought about this passage are these:
  (a) The verses are about a man and his unmarried fiancee.
  (b) The verses are about a father and his unmarried virgin daughter (e.g., "he that giveth her in marriage," v. 38).
Study the paragraph in view of the chapter as a whole, and arrive at your own conclusions as to Paul's intentions here. Commentaries and modern versions may be consulted.

8. *Paragraph 7:39-40.*
Does Paul teach anything new here? How is the paragraph a conclusion to the chapter?

_____

_____

III. NOTES

1. *"Due benevolence"* (7:3). The Berkeley Version reads, "The obligations that are due her."
2. *"I speak this by permission"* (7:6). The word "permission" does not refer to Paul's task of writing but to the Corinthians' marrying. *The Amplified Bible* has this clear rendering: "But I am saying this more as a matter of permission and concession, not as a command or regulation."
3. *"The unbelieving husband is sanctified by the wife"* (7:14). This does not mean that a husband is saved on the basis of his wife's salvation. The reference to "unclean" at the end of 7:14 suggests that Paul had Old Testament background in mind. Johnson comments:

> Paul simply means that the OT principle of the communication of uncleanness does not hold (cf. Hag. 2:11-13). The union is lawful and confers privilege on the members . . . privileges such as the protection of God and the opportunity of being in close contact with one in God's family. This might ease the path of conversion for the unbelieving.[2]

4. *"The present distress"* (7:26). "In view of the troubled times Paul felt it best for men to stay as they were [single or married]. When high seas are raging it is no time for changing ships."[3] Some expositors take it that Paul here is referring to troubles that Christ prophesied would precede His second coming. (Cf. Luke 21:23-28.)

IV. FOR THOUGHT AND DISCUSSION

What are the main teachings of this chapter on the following subjects:

2. See S. Lewis Johnson, "First Corinthians," in *The Wycliffe Bible Commentary*, p. 1240.
3. Leon Morris, *The First Epistle of Paul to the Corinthians*, p. 116.

1. *Marriage*. Who should marry, and when? What are the characteristics and obligations of the married state?

2. *Celibacy*. Who should refrain from marrying and why? What are the characteristics and opportunities of the unmarried state?

3. *Mixed Marriage*. What are the problems of the unequal yoke? What are the obligations of each mate in such a marriage?

4. *Divorce*. What is taught here about divorce?

5. *Remarriage*. What is taught here about remarriage?

V. FURTHER STUDY

You may want to study the full teaching of the New Testament on the subjects of marriage and divorce. For example, include Matthew 5:31-32; 19:3-12 in your study for Christ's teaching about divorce. (See *The New Unger's Bible Dictionary* for articles on the two subjects mentioned above.)

VI. WORDS TO PONDER

Let each one (seek to conduct himself and regulate his affairs so as to) lead the life which the Lord has allotted and imparted to him, and to which God has invited and summoned him (7:17a, *The Amplified Bible*).

Lesson 10

1 Corinthians 8:1–11:1

Boundaries of Christian Liberty

Paul now turns to a question concerning an object or situation that of itself is neutral or nonmoral. The Corinthians' question was, "May we as believers eat meat that has been offered in sacrifice unto idols?" (cf.8:4). Meat, of itself, is neither right nor wrong. But could a Corinthian Christian go to a meat market sponsored by a heathen temple and buy meat that had been left over from a heathen sacrifice? Is this associating oneself anew with the former life of heathenism? Did the Corinthian believer have to consider what other people (especially other believers) would think if he did this, even though both he and God knew that he had no intentions of fellowship in the heathen circle? These were some of the things on Paul's mind as he formulated this lengthy discourse (three chapters in the Bible) on what must have been a stormy issue in the Corinthian congregation. Its application to similar problems of Christian living today is both clear and vital.

I. PREPARATION FOR ANALYSIS

1. Consult a commentary for a description of the procedures followed in Paul's day for the disposition of the animal sacrifices in the heathen temples.[1]
2. Be thinking of situations today where Christians should think twice before acting, even though the deed of itself is neutral.

II. ANALYSIS

Segment to be analyzed: 8:1–11:1
Paragraph divisions: at verses 8:1, 7; 9:1, 15, 19, 24; 10:1, 11, 14, 23

1. For example, see Charles F. Pfeiffer and Everett F. Harrison, eds., *The Wycliffe Bible Commentary*, p. 1241.

80

A. General Analysis

This is a long segment for analysis, but it is important to study the three chapters together in order to see Paul's full answer more clearly. (One study unit could be devoted to the segment as a whole, with the topical study being broken down into a few units.)
1. Read 8:1–11:1 in one sitting. (This may be done in a modern version.) What are your impressions and reactions?

_____

_____

2. Where are there specific references in the segment to eating meat?

_____

_____

_____

Does the passage 9:1–10:13 seem related to this subject?
3. Mark the paragraph divisions in your study version. Then read the segment again, underlining key words and phrases. Record paragraph titles on Chart L.
4. Study the structure of 8:1–11:1 as given on Chart L. From your reading thus far, justify the outlines shown. Add your own observations and outlines to the chart as you continue your study.
5. Does the chart throw any light on the relation of 9:1–10:13 to the entire passage?

_____

6. Why is 11:1 included as part of this segment?

_____

_____

B. Topical Analysis

As you study each topic, refer frequently to Chart L for context reminder.

1. *Problem stated and solution identified in general: 8:1-6.*
Where is the problem stated specifically?

_____

_____

		ATTITUDES EXEMPLIFIED IN PAUL'S MINISTRY						ADMONITIONS	
		selflessness	*subservience*	*subjection*	*Flee from idolatry*			*Forgo your liberty*	
8:1	8:7	9:1 / 9:15	9:19	9:24	10:1	10:11	10:14	10:23	11:1
PROBLEM STATED AND SOLUTION IDENTIFIED IN GENERAL	SOLUTION SPELLED OUT SPECIFICALLY	ATTITUDES THAT ARE BASIC TO THE SOLUTION				ACTIONS THAT ARE THE SOLUTION			
PRINCIPLES STATED		PRINCIPLES ILLUSTRATED				PRINCIPLES APPLIED			

What solutions to the problem are identified in basic principles in the following verses?
8:1*b*-2

_____

8:3

_____

8:4-6

_____

2. *Solution spelled out specifically: 8:7-13.*
Record below the various descriptions or identifications given of
the two kinds of Christians:

the strong Christian	the weaker Christian

Observe the references to *knowledge* in the paragraph. Recall the
prominence of this subject in 8:1-6. When Paul refers to knowledge, he means knowledge of what?

_____

_____

Who is the one with this knowledge?

_____

_____

Analyze carefully the key phrase: "*liberty* of yours BECOME a
stumblingblock to them" (8:9). How does Paul bring Christ into
the solution?

_____

_____

What does verse 13 add to your answer of this question?

_____

3. *Attitudes that are basic to the solution: 9:1-27.*
(a) *Selflessness* (9:1-14; 15-18).
Analyze the two paragraphs around this fourfold thread (mark the
phrases prominently in your Bible):
    "Have we not power to ... ?" (9:4)
    "Nevertheless we have not used this power" (9:12)

"But I have used none of these things" (9:15)
"That I abuse not my power" (9:18)
What basically are the two facts Paul is establishing in this passage?

_____

_____

How does this relate to the problem stated in chapter 8?

_____

_____

What was there about Paul's position in the Christian community of the Mediterranean "world" that made it necessary and advantageous for him to be independent of any salary arrangement in his preaching ministry? (Note: For a clearer rendering of 9:17, consult a modern version.)

_____

What different examples of selflessness do you see here?

_____

_____

(b) *Subservience* (9:19-23).
Compare "servant unto" (v. 19) and "partaker . . . with" (v. 23).

_____

_____

How is the relationship of subservience a solution to the problem of chapter 8?

_____

(c) *Subjection (discipline)* (9:24-27).
What truths about discipline are taught here?

_____

_____

How does such discipline help a Christian avoid being a stumbling block to a weaker brother?

_____

4. *Actions that are the solution: 10:1–11:1.*
(a) *Flee from idolatry* (10:1-22).
Recall your three paragraph titles for this passage. Read the paragraphs again in the light of the key verse 14.
(1) *Paragraph 10:1-10.* Here is a good example of how contemporary the Scriptures are to any era. Paul applies Old Testament

history to his own times (modern from his standpoint). Record his illustrations:

Israelites' Spiritual Position and Participation (10:1-4)	Israelites' Sins (10:6-10)	Israelites' Punishment (10:5; 8-10)

What is Paul's main plea in this paragraph?

_____

_____

How is this paragraph, with its many references to moral situations (e.g., fornication), related to the original problem of chapter 8 about a nonmoral situation?

_____

_____

(2) *Paragraph 10:11-13*. What is the exhortation here?

_____

Why does Paul add the encouragement of verse 13 at this point?

_____

_____

(3) *Paragraph 10:14-22*. On first reading, this paragraph appears very complicated, until a pattern appears. Paul here is describing three entirely different altar experiences, which illustrate the truth that a man is known by the one altar of which he partakes. Observe the repetition of the word "partake" (and similar words) in the paragraph. Identify the three altars:

10:16-17

_____

10:18

_____

10:19-21

_____

What various truths does Paul derive from these three illustrations?

_____

_____

_____

_____

Again, what is his main point?

_____

(b) *Forgo your liberty* (10:23–11:1).
This is the final paragraph in the section. It is an appropriate conclusion, for Paul refers specifically to the problem as originally stated in chapter 8, that of eating meat that had been offered in a heathen sacrifice. Make a list of the different motivations for Christian action cited in the paragraph. (On 10:23, review your earlier study of 6:12.)

III. NOTES

1. *"Their conscience being weak is defiled"* (8:7). Many of the Corinthian Christians were needlessly hindering their spiritual growth because they did not have a true perspective of the meat-eating situation. Bruce's expanded paraphrase of 8:7 brings this out clearly:

> Yet this clear knowledge is not enjoyed by all. Some, Christians though they are, through force of habit and familiarity with the idea of the idol, still regard such food, when they eat it, as having been sacrificed to an idol. They have a tender conscience in this matter, and it is stained with a sense of guilt if they ignore it and eat the food.

2. *"That Rock was Christ"* (10:4*b*). Paul here clearly teaches that the preincarnate Christ was the source of spiritual blessings in Old Testament days. (Read John 1:1-5 for perspective here.)

3. *"For why is my liberty judged of another man's con-science?"* (10:29). *The Living Bible* reads, "But why, you may ask, must I be guided and limited by what someone else thinks?" The question is restated in verse 30 and is answered in verses 31-33.

4. *" Shambles"* (10:25). The Greek word means literally "shop," translated "meat market" in the Berkeley Version.

IV. FOR THOUGHT AND DISCUSSION

1. What specific situations in Christian living today are similar to the meat-eating problem of these messages? Do the basic principles of a solution remain unchanged?

2. Why do pride and selfishness kill any solution to the problem? Apply the phrase "[Love] seeketh not her own" (13:5) to this. Evaluate this statement: "Love says someone is watching."

3. Are obligations and liberty unmixables? Support your answer by the teachings of this passage, and illustrate it by examples in present-day life.

4. What various doctrines are taught in 8:6?

5. Write a list of the main spiritual lessons taught in 8:1–11:1.

V. FURTHER STUDY

Two subjects suggested for extended study are:

1. The doctrine of Christian liberty taught in the epistle to the Galatians.

2. The relationship of the first and second commandments (see Matt. 22:34-40) to the teachings of 1 Corinthians 8:1–11:1.

VI. WORDS TO PONDER

To win the contest you must deny yourselves many things that would keep you from doing your best (9:25a, *The Living Bible*).

Lesson 11

1 Corinthians 11:2-34

Two Problems About the Worship Service

Problems of the congregation as a whole—in their worship services—are now discussed by Paul. Chart M shows this context of this lesson.

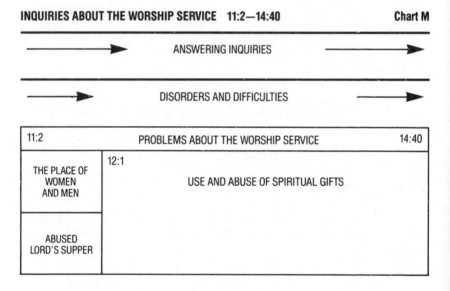

INQUIRIES ABOUT THE WORSHIP SERVICE   11:2—14:40   **Chart M**

———————→   ANSWERING INQUIRIES   ———————→

——————→   DISORDERS AND DIFFICULTIES   ——————→

11:2	PROBLEMS ABOUT THE WORSHIP SERVICE	14:40
THE PLACE OF WOMEN AND MEN	12:1 USE AND ABUSE OF SPIRITUAL GIFTS	
ABUSED LORD'S SUPPER		

The questions Paul answers in chapter 11 are about the worship service. We do not know exactly how the Corinthian inquirers worded their questions, but from Paul's answers we can conclude rather accurately what the questions were. An important observation is that some of the Corinthian Christians were deeply concerned about guarding the sanctity of their public worship. Hence their appeal to Paul.

I. PREPARATION FOR ANALYSIS

1. Consult a Bible dictionary for descriptions of these two items of Paul's day:
   (a) *Love feast.* This was a full-course meal observed before, but in connection with, the Lord's Supper. Read Jude 12 and 2 Peter 2:13 (see ASV marginal note).
   (b) *Woman's veil.* A Bible dictionary usually refers to the subject "dress" for this.
2. Read Genesis 1: 26-27 and 2:21-25 concerning man and woman in the creation account.
3. Read the gospel accounts of the origin of the Lord's Supper: Matthew 26:26-29; Mark 14:22-25; Luke 22:14-20.

II. ANALYSIS

Segments to be analyzed: 11:2-16 and 11:17-34.
Paragraph divisions: at verses 2, 17, 23, 27, 33.

A. The Place of Women and Men in the Worship Service: 11:2-16

1. Read the passage for general impressions. How often do these two sets appear here: woman and man; covered and uncovered head? Concentrate your analysis on these.
2. Observe and study every reference to Christ and God in the passage.
3. According to Paul, what should be preeminent in all worship services?

_____

_____

Let this be the key determinant in your interpretations of the details of the passage.
4. Paul cites at least three arguments for the standard of head covering in the worship service:
(a) *Nature.* What verses refer to this?

_____

_____

What is Paul's argument?

_____

_____

(b) *Social standards.* The "shorn" (v. 6) or shaven woman of Paul's day was known by all as an adulteress. Observe how Paul refers to this only as an illustration (in ultimate degree) of his argument for a head covering.

(c) *Symbolic teaching.* Most of Paul's argument is via symbolic teaching. The prominent symbol here is the head covering. Covering is a symbol of subjection, of keeping down. The opposite symbol, uncovering, means magnifying, exalting. Study Chart N, observing these symbols.

5. Observe the following in connection with the chart:

(a) Note the three prominent sets: woman and man, covered head and uncovered head, glory of man and glory of God.

(b) Read 11: 2-16 slowly, and observe how each point of each verse is represented on the chart.

(c) Paul recognizes *equality* in *status* but *differences* in *function* in God's creations of man and woman.[1] How is this illustrated in the Trinity?

_____

_____

(d) Whose glory should shine forth in a worship service?

_____

How is this represented on the chart? How does the passage support this progression:

    A woman's hair is her glory.
    A woman is man's glory.
    There is a higher glory—the glory of God.

(e) Do you think the outward appearance of a woman was the only material item that could lend support to the true spirit of worship in Paul's day?

_____

_____

B. The Right Way to Observe the Lord's Supper: 11:17-34.

The right observance of the Lord's Supper depends on a correct view of the origin, meaning, and purpose of this ordinance.[2] The key paragraph of this segment is 11:23-26, which describes the ordinance itself. Study this paragraph carefully, and then study its surrounding paragraphs (11:17-22 and 11:27-32) in light of its

1. Cf. Gal. 3:28; Eph. 1:3.
2. Cf. 11:2*b*.

90

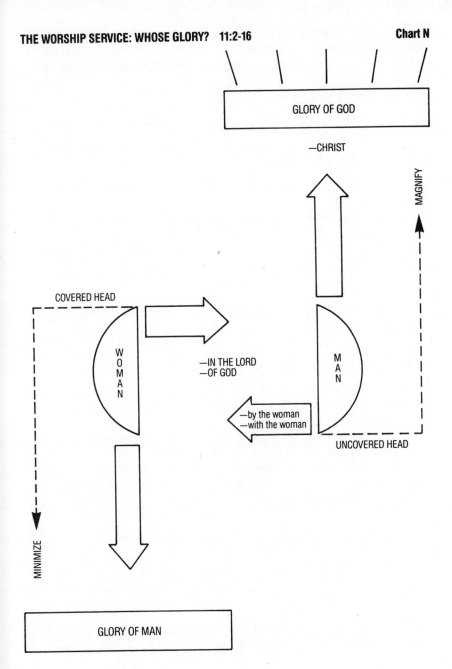

91

teachings. What are the problems of the two latter paragraphs, and how are answers established in 11:23-26? Record your observations below. (Note: Paragraph 11:33-34 is a summary to the segment.)

1. *Paragraph 11:17-22: The Abuse.*

2. *Paragraph 11:23-26: The Ordinance.*

3. *Paragraph 11:27-32: The Participants.*

4. *Paragraph 11:33-34: Summary.*

III. NOTES

1. *"Prophesying"* (11:4). Paul discusses the gift of prophecy at length in chapter 14. Ministries of forthtelling (e.g., teaching and preaching) and foretelling are both involved.
2. *"Power on her head"* (11:10a). The phrase means "token of authority on her head" (Berkeley).
3. *"Because of the angels"* (11:10b. All expositors recognize the difficulty in identifying the intention of this phrase. *The New Bible Commentary* writes:

> A simpler interpretation is to see here a reference to the fact that the Jews and the early Christian Church thought of angels as being present in their worshipping assemblies. Where they in all their holy order are assembled, recognition of the divinely constituted order of creation should be shown by every worshipper.[3]

4. *"If a man have long hair, it is a shame unto him"* (11:14). Some groups in Paul's day, as in all cultures and ages, favored

---

3. W. C. G. Proctor, "1 Corinthians: Commentary," in *The New Bible Commentary*, p. 983.

long hair for men. But generally speaking, it was looked down upon by the populace.

5. *"Divisions among you"* (11:18). The reference to "hungry" people (11:21) and "them that have not" (11:22) suggests at least two main parties ("divisions") in the Corinthian church: the rich and the poor. The rich people apparently arrived at the church early and began to eat the food of the love feast *(agape)* without waiting for the poor (many of whom were servants) to arrive (cf. 11:21, 33). Their motive was gluttony (11:21, 34) and, deeper yet, pride (11:19). They probably did not want to be visibly identified with the poor in the church. And yet one of the characteristics of the Lord's Supper that followed the love feast was a unity of believers (cf. 11:33).

6. *"Unworthily"* (11:27). The word has reference to the *manner* of observing the Lord's Supper. One way to be guilty of this is by "not discerning the Lord's body" (11:29), that is, not recognizing the full worth of the death of Christ. "Such an unworthy use the Corinthians made of the Communion when they served it after a love feast marred by quarrels."[4]

IV. FOR THOUGHT AND DISCUSSION

What are some of the main *timeless, universal* truths that you have learned in this chapter of *local* setting? Apply these universal truths to the local setting of your own church. Think especially about the two situations of the chapter: the place of women and men in the worship service, and the correct way to participate in the Lord's Supper (eucharist).

V. FURTHER STUDY

Two subjects recommended for extended study are:
1. The full New Testament teaching on the place of women in the church
2. A word study of "glory" in the Old and New Testaments.

VI. WORDS TO PONDER

Every time you eat this bread and drink the cup you proclaim the death of the Lord, and continue to do so until He comes (11:26, Bruce's *Expanded Paraphrase*).

---

4. F.W. Grosheide, *Commentary on the First Epistle to the Corinthians*, pp. 273-74.

Lesson 12

Spiritual Gifts

Chapters 12 to 14 teach indispensable truths about the actual operations of the church in its gospel ministry. *Diversity in unity* is the theme here, very concisely stated by 12:6: "There are diversities of operations, but it is the same God which worketh all in all."

The three chapters of this lessons clearly form a unit:

Chapter 12 is about "spiritual gifts," or divinely endowed capacities for service.

Chapter 14 compares two of these gifts (prophecy and tongues).

Chapter 13 is the classic treatise on "love," the grace that makes gifts fruitful.

Read 14:1, and observe how the subjects of each of the three chapters are represented by the verse:

"Follow after love,	and desire spiritual gifts,	but rather that ye may prophesy." (14:1)
chap. 13	chap. 12	chap. 14

Because of the length of the Scripture passage, you would do best to divide the lesson into three study units, one chapter per unit.

INTRODUCTION

1

I would not have you ignorant

JESUS IS THE LORD

appeal for
KNOWLEDGE

DIVINE DESIGN OF THE CHURCH'S MINISTRY

ONE
SOURCE

—preeminence of
GOD'S WAY

4

ONE
BODY

—preeminence of
CHRIST

12

MANY
MEMBERS

—honor of the
INDIVIDUAL

14

many gifts

ONE
CHURCH

many gifts

SUMMARY

27

covet earnestly

—and yet show I unto you

A MORE EXCELLENT WAY

31

appeal for
ASPIRATION

Chap. 13

95

I. PREPARATION FOR ANALYSIS

1. The lists of gifts found in chapter 12 are not exhaustive. Read Romans 12:68 and Ephesians 4:11, and keep these lists in mind as you study 1 Corinthians 12. (See *Further Study* below for other New Testament references to spiritual gifts.)

2. Before studying chapter 14, read these passages, most of which record actual instances of speaking in "tongues": Mark 16:17; Acts 2:1-13; 10:44-46; 19:6. Then read descriptions and explanations of this phenomena in an outside source such as a Bible dictionary.[1] Note that there are two different views as to the exact nature of the Corinthian tongues: (1) they were the same kind of utterances such as were spoken on the day of Pentecost (Acts 2:1-13), that is, languages foreign and unintelligible to the speakers but native and intelligible to the hearers, and (2) they were ecstatic utterances of a nonexisting language understood by the listeners only through an interpreter.

II. ANALYSIS

Segments to be analyzed: 12:1-31; 13:1-13; 14:1-40
Paragraph divisions: at verses 12:1, 4, 12, 14, 27; 13:1, 4, 8; 14:1, 6, 13, 20, 26, 33*b*, 37

Follow procedures of analysis suggested in the earlier lessons of this manual. Keep training your eyes to see; use your pencil continuously; arrive at sound interpretations; and be honest in applying the Scripture to your own life.

A. Chapter 12: Spiritual Gifts in the Ministry of the Church

Chart O is a partially completed analytical chart. Use it to suggest various lines of study. Add your own observations to it.
1. *Introduction: 12:1-3.*
What contrast is made between the before and the after?

_____

_____

---

1. E.g., Merrill C. Tenney, *Zondervan Pictorial Bible Dictionary*, pp. 859-60; Merrill F. Unger, *Unger's Bible Dictionary*, pp. 1107-8; John F. Walvoord, *The Holy Spirit* (Grand Rapids: Zondervan, 1958), pp. 180ff.

What is the central doctrine of the church's ministry?

_____

_____

Who is the infallible interpreter of the church's message?

_____

_____

Do you see any connection between 12:2-3 and the phrase "spiritual gifts"[2] (12:1)?
2. *One source: 12:4-11.*
Note the repeated phrase "same Spirit" in this paragraph. What does this emphasize?

_____

_____

Note also the words "gifts" and "given." Analyze the three statements of 12:4-6. Note the Trinity. What is meant by each of the gifts of 12:8-10? Compare the list with 12:28-30. How is the distribution of gifts determined (12:11)? (Cf. 12:18, 28.)

_____

_____

3. *One body: 12:12-13.*
What important truths are taught here?

_____

_____

4. *Many members: 12:14-26.*
What applications to Christian service do you see in this paragraph?

_____

_____

5. *Summary: 12:27-31.*
In view of divine sovereignty, how do you reconcile these two statements concerning spiritual gifts:

2. Observe that the word "gifts" of 12:1 is not in the original Greek text (hence the word is italicized in most Bibles). The added explanatory word is justified in view of the context.

"God hath set" (12:28)   "[You] covet earnestly (12:31)
      (GOD'S PART)   (YOUR PART)

Why should Christians "covet earnestly the best gifts" (12:31)?

_____

_____

What does the concluding phrase of 12:31 do for the whole chapter?

_____

How does it relate to chapter 13?

_____

_____

B. Chapter 13: Love

Henry Alford writes of this chapter on love[3] as "a pure and perfect gem, perhaps the noblest assemblage of beautiful thoughts in beautiful language extant in this our world."[4] Another writer reconstructs this scene when Paul wrote the masterpiece:

> We can imagine how the apostle's amanuensis must have paused to look up in his master's face at the sudden change of his style of dictation, and seen his countenance lighted up as it had been the face of an angel, as the sublime vision of divine perfection passed before him.[5]

All will agree that the beauty of this literary masterpiece is excelled by the importance of its message. Analyze the chapter slowly and carefully, phrase by phrase. Watch for groupings and progressions in the lists, to help you feel and understand all that Paul, inspired by the Spirit, is trying to say. An efficient way to record your study is to write the text, phrase by phrase, on the left-hand side of a piece of paper, and observations and interpretations on the right-hand side, opposite the text.

---

3. "Love" is a better translation of the Greek *agape* than the King James Version's "charity." The latter word today has a narrower, specialized connotation of *deeds* of love (cf. 13:3*a*.) In translating the Greek into Latin, Jerome preferred *caritas* over *amor*, to avoid what he thought was a sensual connotation in the latter. Wycliffe followed through on Jerome's *caritas* with "charity," thence the King James translation.
4. Henry Alford, *The Greek Testament*, 2:57.
5. Dean Stanley as quoted in ibid, p. 585.

An outline suggested for this three-paragraph chapter is this:

Values of love	(13:1-3)	–shown by its absence
Characteristics of Love	(13:4-7)	–shown by its presence
Abiding Nature of Love	(13:8-13)	–shown by comparison

After you have completed your analysis, answer these three questions:

1. What is the main point of this chapter, in your own words?

_____

_____

2. What does verse 13 teach? Weigh this comment, "Love is at once the strength of faith and the inspiration of hope."[6]

3. How is this chapter related to its surrounding chapters?

_____

_____

Try writing out your own reflections on the superlative quality of love as measured by 1 Corinthians 13. Include the excelling and distinctive characteristic of love that relates the Christian to other persons. John Calvin noted in his commentary on 1 Corinthians, "Each person derives personal blessing from his own faith and hope, whereas love is poured out for the good of others."

C. Chapter 14: Tongues and Prophecy Compared

In this chapter Paul compares two spiritual gifts that were being exercised in the church at Corinth. (See Notes for a discussion of temporary and permanent spiritual gifts.) Although the gifts are claimed by only a small part of the church today, the principles and truths they embody, because these are timeless, make this chapter vitally contemporary. Thus we want to study the chapter with present-day applications in mind.

Definitions are in order concerning the two gifts of chapter 14: (1) gift of prophecy—the divine gift of revealing the will of God, meeting the need that later was to be filled by the written New Testament, and (2) gift of tongues—the divine gift of express-

6. G. Campbell Morgan, *The Corinthian Letters of Paul*, p. 109.

ing praises to God in words[7] unintelligible to the hearers. The words are intelligible to those who have been given the gift of interpretation (12:10).

The structure of the chapter is shown by Chart P. Mark these divisions in your Bible, as well as paragraph divisions.

Read the chapter through once, underlining strong words and repeated words. Note, for example, every reference to edification. What is the main point of each paragraph? Compare your observations on this with the keynotes shown on Chart P.

The first four paragraphs (14:1-25) compare the gifts of speaking in tongues and prophesying, and show how the latter gift excels.[8] Analyze each paragraph, and record the comparisons on Chart P, similar to the example shown.

The two paragraphs of 14:26-36 give instructions as to the order of the worship service, especially with reference to the two spiritual gifts. Record these instructions on Chart P.

How does the last paragraph conclude the chapter?

_____

_____

What does the last verse suggest as to what may have been a problem in the Corinthian church?

_____

_____

As a concluding exercise, list what you consider to be ten important truths about public worship taught by this chapter.

_____

_____

_____

_____

_____

_____

_____

_____

7. As noted earlier, the tongues of Pentecost were of languages of the world. If the Corinthian tongues were not ecstatic utterances, they were not necessarily of languages of the world. Marvin R. Vincent says, "It does not necessarily mean any of the known languages of men, but may mean the speaker's own tongue, shaped in a peculiar manner by the Spirit's influence; or an entirely new spiritual language" (*Word Studies in the New Testament*, 3:257).
8. Observe in the lists of chap. 12 how the gift of tongues is always cited last: 12:10, 28, 30.

III. NOTES

1. *"Diversities of gifts"* (12:4). The spiritual gifts may be classified as either permanent (lasting through the church age) or temporary not generally given by God after the early church had its credentials in the written New Testament). The main temporary gifts are: apostleship, prophecy, miracles, healing, tongues, and interpreting tongues. The other gifts are permanent (e.g., teaching, helps, governments, 12:28).

John F. Walvoord writes this about the withdrawal of temporary gifts from the church as a whole:

> The best explanation of the passing of certain gifts and their manifestation is found in the evident purpose of God in the apostolic age. During the lifetime of the apostles, it pleased God to perform many notable miracles, in some cases quite apart from the question of whether the benefit was deserved. A period of miracles is always a time when special testimony is needed to the authenticity of God's prophets.[9]

2. *"Discerning of spirits"* (12:10). This is the distinguishing between the false and the true in the spirit world.

3. *"Covet earnestly the best gifts"* (12:31). In saying this Paul wants to avoid stifling ambition and aspiration. He does not expect all to have the "best" or "greater") gifts, in view of what he has just said in 12:28-30.

4. *"A more excellent way"* (12:31). Paul is not here listing love as another spiritual gift. In effect he is saying, "In your exercise of these gifts, be sure you keep traveling on the pathway of love."

5. *"Puffed up"* (13:4) The Greek word appears six times in 1 Corinthians 4:6, 18, 19; 5:2; 8:1; 13:4 and once in Colossians 2:18. What does this reveal about the Corinthians?

6. *"Believeth all things"* (13:7). Morris comments, "It is easy to think the worst, but love retains its faith. It is not implied that love is deceived by the pretences of any rougue, but that love is always ready to give the benefit of the doubt."[10]

7. *"Let your women keep silence in the churches"* (14:34). G. Coleman Luck comments, "As already seen in chapter 7, unruly and self-assertive women were causing trouble in the Corinthian assembly. The present reference is to wives not chattering in

9. Walvoord, p. 173. Read pp. 163-88 for a full discussion of permanent and spiritual gifts.
10. Leon Morris, *The First Epistle of Paul to the Corinthians*, p. 185.

"LET ALL THINGS BE DONE UNTO EDIFYING" (14:26b) 14:1-40

KEYNOTES →

edification	clarity	spirit and understanding	the hearers	
14:1	6	13	20	26	33b	37	40

| TONGUES AND PROPHECY COMPARED | ORDER AND PROCEDURE IN THE WORSHIP SERVICE | SUMMARY |

TONGUES	PROPHECY
1. directed to God	1. directed to people
2. content: mysteries	2. content: edification exhortation comfort
3. edification: self	3. edification: church

102

church but rather speaking quietly with their husbands at a later time, if they have any real question."[11]

IV. FOR THOUGHT AND DISCUSSION

1. "Every believer possesses a spiritual gift, but not all believers possess the same gift."[12] If this is true, what gift is yours? Do you think that some spiritual gifts are not included in the lists recorded in the Bible?
2. Think of how you might paraphrase 1 Corinthians 13 in the context of a particular situation in your own life. The following missionary's paraphrase of verses 1-3c serves as an example:

> If I speak with the tongues of nationals and of senior missionaries, but have not love, I am become a blaring trumpet or a clanging cymbal.
> And if I have great administrative ability, and understand all doctrines and all customs; and if I have all faith so as to remove obstinate government officials, but have not love, I am nothing.
> And if I give up all the comforts of the homeland to minister to the heathen, and if I am martyred on the field, but have not love, it profiteth me nothing.
> Love is patient and kind to fellow missionaries; love is not envious of another's support; love does not boast of many deputation meetings, is not inflated with pride;
> Does not become arrogant to fellow workers, does not insist on its own methods, is not provoked by trying personalities, takes no thought of self;
> Rejoices not in the shortcomings of others, but rejoices in their triumphs;
> Bears all the hardships of the life, believes even when everything goes wrong, hopes in the "hopeless" situations, endures through everything.
> Love never fails.[13]

3. If you are studying in a group, discuss ways to make a public worship service more edifying to the worshiper.

---

11. G. Coleman Luck, *First Corinthians*, p. 111.
12. Charles F. Pfeiffer and Everett F. Harrison, eds., *The Wycliffe Bible Commentary*, p. 1249.
13. Paraphrase by Charles Willoughby in a tract, "A Missionary Paraphrase of 1 Corinthians 13" (Chicago: The Evangelical Alliance Mission).

V. FURTHER STUDY

1. Extend your study of spiritual gifts to include these passages: Romans 1: 11; 1 Peter 4:10; Romans 12:6; 1 Corinthians 4:7; 2 Timothy 1:6; Hebrews 2:4.

2. Study further the gift of tongues-speaking (glossolalia), as to these areas:

(a) The false and the true

(b) Temporary or permanent

(c) Recent spread of the tongues movement to denominations not affiliated with "holiness" groups

Various books and articles are available on this subject.

3. Study the gospels for Christ's teachings on love (e.g., Mark 12:28-34; in 15:12).

VI. WORDS TO PONDER

Seek that ye may excel to the edifying of the church (14:12*b*).

Lesson 13

1 Corinthians 15:1-58

The Resurrection Chapter

Paul discusses the resurrection last to emphasize that its truth makes all human problems solvable. Death, of course, is man's greatest "problem." One prominent U.S. Senator, on returning to Washington after treatment for cancer, reflected that "no one really grows up until he realizes he has to die." But such a sobering thought is not a saving thing, for the man's predicament remains unsolved: he wants to live, but he must die. This is where the gospel of resurrection comes in, offering man's only hope: "in Christ shall all be made alive" (15:22). Morgan's comment is true: "The glory of our Christianity is that it never views life as being complete in this world."[1]

When the Corinthians asked Paul questions about the resurrection, the apostle surely diagnosed these doubts as a main root of all their other problems. Thus his conclusion to the resurrection chapter is also a conclusion to all the preceding chapters about problems. And what a triumphant conclusion it is:

> Thanks be to God, which giveth us the victory through our Lord Jesus Christ. Therefore, my beloved brethren, be ye stedfast, unmoveable, always abounding in the work of the Lord, forasmuch as ye know that your labour is not in vain in the Lord (15:57-58).

I. PREPARATION FOR STUDY

1. Read the historical record of the empty tomb and the risen Christ in any of the four gospels (e.g., John 20). Read also Matthew 27:62-66, observing how the religious rulers denied Christ's resurrection before the day of resurrection (third day) even arrived.

1. G. Campbell Morgan, *The Corinthian Letters of Paul*, p. 120.

105

2. It may surprise you that the Corinthians would have such doubts about the bodily resurrection of saints. The following background of the Greek view of life will help to explain the existence of such a problem:

> In general the Greeks believed in the immortality of the soul, but they did not accept the resurrection of the body. To them the resurrection of the body was unthinkable in view of the fact that they held the body to be the source of man's weakness and sin. Death, therefore, was very welcome, since by it the soul would be liberated from the body; but resurrection was not welcome, because this would constitute another descent of the soul into the grave of the body.[2]

3. Reflect on the relationship between an Easter faith (belief in a risen Christ) and the Easter fact (truth of Christ's literal bodily resurrection from the tomb). Some people think there can be an Easter faith without the Easter fact. What do you think?

II. ANALYSIS

Segments to be analyzed: 15:1-34 and 35-58
Paragraph divisions: at verses 1, 12, 20, 29, 35, 39, 50, 58

A. General Analysis

1. Observe on Chart Q how the chapter is divided into two main parts, answering two main questions. Keep this chart before you as you analyze each paragraph, recording your observations in the appropriate paragraph boxes.
2. How is the last verse, coupled with verse 57, a practical conclusion to this chapter?

B. Paragraph Analysis

Analyze the text paragraph by paragraph, using study procedures and recording methods suggested in the previous lessons. For each paragraph be sure to look for (1) the main point of each

---

2. S. Lewis Johnson, "First Corinthians," in *The Wycliffe Bible Commentary*, p. 1255. Among the Greek philosophers, Epicureans denied any existence beyond death; Stoics held that death brought a merging of the soul in deity, and so a loss of personality; Platonists absolutely denied bodily resurrection. It is possible also that some of the Jewish converts of the Corinthian church had been influenced by the Sadducees' denial of resurrection (cf. Acts 23:8).

paragraph, (2) key words and phrases, and (3) important doctrines and practical lessons.

III. NOTES

1. *"Christ died for our sins according to the scriptures"* (15:3). When Paul wrote this, the Scriptures were the scrolls of the Old Testament. Passages clearly foretelling the death of Christ included Psalm 22 and Isaiah 53.

2. *"In Adam . . . in Christ"* (15:22). The contrast of Adam and Christ is a favorite subject in Paul's writings. Read Romans 5:12-19 (cf. Eph 4:22-24; Col. 3:8-11).

3. *"Then shall the Son also himself be subject unto him [the Father]"* (15:28). This is subordination of office, respecting the functions of Son and Father. Christ's deity is not denied by such a relationship.

4. *"Baptized for the dead"* (15:29). Most expositors agree that it is diiiicult to determine which of various possible meanings is intended here. Such possible meanings include:

(a) Baptism on the basis of the testimony of some who had died[3]

(b) Baptism of young converts who took the place in the church of older brethren who had died

(c) A custom practiced by some in Paul's day,[4] for reasons unknown to us, which Paul cites to illustrate his argument, but which he does not defend[5]

IV. FOR THOUGHT AND DISCUSSION

1. What truths of chapter 15 are guides in the solutions of the problems cited earlier in the epistle? For examples, refer to the bottom of survey Chart C.

2. What various proofs of Christ's resurrection does Paul cite? Can you add to this list?

3. Evaluate the interpretation that Christ's resurrection demonstrated (1) the perfection of Christ's character (Acts 2:24) and (2) the Father's acceptance of His death as substitutionary for the sins of the whole world. (Rom. 4:25)

4. In your own words, what kind of a body will you as a believer have in heaven? (Read Luke 24:29-43; Phil. 3:21; Ps. 17:15,

---

3. See ibid., p. 1257.
4. Note how the pronoun changes from "they" in v. 29 to "we" in v. 30.
5. G. Campbell Morgan prefers this view.

THE RESURRECTION CHAPTER (15:1-58)

Chart Q

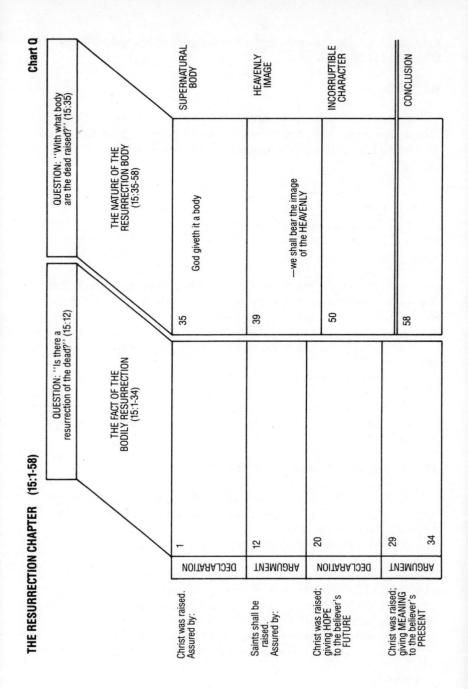

	QUESTION: "Is there a resurrection of the dead?" (15:12)	QUESTION: "With what body are the dead raised?" (15:35)
	THE FACT OF THE BODILY RESURRECTION (15:1-34)	THE NATURE OF THE RESURRECTION BODY (15:35-58)

Nature of the Resurrection Body section:

Verse		Topic
35	God giveth it a body	SUPERNATURAL BODY
39	—we shall bear the image of the HEAVENLY	HEAVENLY IMAGE
50		INCORRUPTIBLE CHARACTER
58		CONCLUSION

Fact of the Bodily Resurrection section:

Verse	Type	
1	DECLARATION	Christ was raised. Assured by:
12	ARGUMENT	Saints shall be raised. Assured by:
20	DECLARATION	Christ was raised; giving HOPE to the believer's FUTURE
29 / 34	ARGUMENT	Christ was raised; giving MEANING to the believer's PRESENT

108

and consider such descriptions as those of continuity, identity, and diversity in 1 Cor. 15.)

V. FURTHER STUDY

Three theories that have been advanced denying the resurrection of Jesus' body are the Swoon, Fraud, and Phantom theories. Consult outside sources for a discussion of these false views.

VI. WORDS TO PONDER

That ye may know
what is the exceeding greatness of his POWER
    [dynamite] to us-ward who believe,
according to that WORKING [energy]
of the STRENGTH of his MIGHT
which he WROUGHT [exercisedl in Christ
when he
    RAISED HIM FROM THE DEAD
and set him at his own right hand (Eph. 1:18-20).

Lesson 14

A Fellowship of Christians in Action

This last chapter of 1 Corinthians, written in casual and informal style, serves many purposes. There are personal greetings, announcements, and a warm "Good-bye, I'll be seeing you." There are practical lessons, and even a few doctrines. The whole chapter is typical of a conclusion to a Pauline epistle.

The peak of Paul's message to the Corinthians is the last verse of chapter 15 (15:58). That verse concludes the peak chapter of the epistle, the resurrection discourse. Now in the last chapter Paul relaxes, as it were. He has committed the discussed problems hopefully to a confrontation between the Corinthians and the Lord. There is nothing now to hinder a continued warm fellowship with the very brothers and sisters in Christ he has just reproved. Chapter 16 shows that unbroken fellowship in action. Study the chapter carefully, and you will agree that it is a vital part of the entire epistle.

I. PREPARATION FOR STUDY

1. Read 2 Corintaians 8:1–9:15 for a longer discussion of the freewill offering Paul was collecting for the needy saints in Jerusalem (16:1).

2. Review the salutation of 1 Corinthians (1:1-9), and keep this in mind as you study the concluding chapter of Paul's letter. Do you think that Paul may have penned these introductory words (1:1-9) after he had completed the epistle, just as an author today usually writes the introduction to his book after he has written everything else?

II. ANALYSIS

Segment to be analyzed: 16:1-24
Paragraph divisions: at verses 1, 5, 10, 12, 13, 15, 19, 21

1. The contents of this final chapter are varied, which suggests that there are various ways to study it. Read the chapter once for general impressions.
2. Return to it a few more times, observing references to the following subjects:
(a) Geographical places

___

(b) Different local churches

___

(c) Christian leaders and laymen

___

(d) Every appearance of the word "come"

___

(e) Future plans of Paul

___

The above study will acquaint you with the local setting of the chapter.
3. Now spend time studying the following important doctrinal and practical subjects. Record what the chapter teaches about each:
(a) *The fellowship of the church*

___

(b) *Christian service.* Observe how chapter 16 illustrates the "work" and "labor" of 15:58.)

___

(c) *Kindness and liberality*

___

III. NOTES

1. *"First day of the week"* (16:2). This is the earliest reference in the New Testament to Sunday as the church's day of worship. Compare Acts 20:7.

2. *"Holy kiss"* (16:20). Greeting by a kiss was a custom in Eastern lands in Paul's day (as it is today). The church used the phrase "holy kiss" as a symbol of Christian greeting. (See Rom. 16:16; 1 Thess. 5:26; 2 Cor. 13:12; 1 Pet.5:14.)

3. *"Anathema"* (16:22). The word means "accursed." Compare Romans 9:3; Galatians 1:8-9; 1 Corinthians 12:3. (Note: There should be a period in the Bible text after the word "Anathema.")

4. *"Maranatha"* (16:22). This Aramaic term represents a full English sentence. Actually, any of these readings is possible: "O our Lord, come;" "Our Lord is [or has] come" (incarnation); "Our Lord cometh" (second coming).

IV. FOR THOUGHT AND DISCUSSION

Read the chapter one more time, observing how the passage is related to all the preceding "problem" chapters by virtue of the fact that it makes no reference to problems.

SUMMARY

"No epistle tells us this much about the life of a primitive local church." In 1 Corinthians Paul makes an honest diagnosis of the young church at Corinth, and he shows solutions and shares testimony so that this young congregation he founded can be restored to its former spiritual health.

The problems of the congregation as a group included disunity, sophisticated intellectualism, neglect of discipline of its members, evil fellowships, and civil lawsuits. These were the problems "reported" to Paul by concerned believers in the church (1: 10–6:20).

Then there were personal problems of the individual members, about which the church wrote Paul for his counsel (7:1–15:58). These involved the responsibilities of marriage, the question of whether to marry or not to marry, and whether to eat meat that had been sacrificed to idols. Paul also answered questions about the worship service, specifically about the place of man and woman in the service, abuses of the Lord's table, and an evaluation of spiritual gifts in the ministry of the gospel.

Paul devoted the last chapter (15) of the main body of his epistle to the cardinal doctrine of the Christian faith: the resurrection. Every church has its problems, but what about man's most desperate plight—the appointment with death? "Resurrection in Christ" (15:22) is Paul's answer, and it is this truth that brings the apostle to the peak of the epistle in the praise "Thanks be to God, which giveth us the victory through our Lord Jesus Christ" (15:57), coupled with the appeal to be "stedfast, unmoveable, always abounding in the work of the Lord" (15:58).

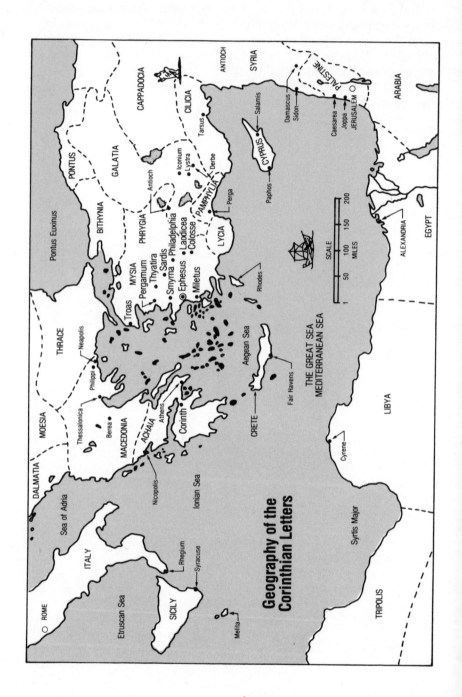

Geography of the Corinthian Letters

ANTIOCH
SYRIA
PALESTINE
ARABIA
CAPPADOCIA
CILICIA
Salamis
Damascus
Sidon
Caesarea
Joppa
JERUSALEM
Tarsus
CYPRUS
Paphos
PONTUS
GALATIA
Antioch
Iconium
Lystra
Derbe
Perga
PAMPHYLIA
EGYPT
BITHYNIA
PHRYGIA
Philadelphia
LYCIA
ALEXANDRIA
Pontus Euxinus
MYSIA
Pergamum
Thyatira
Sardis
Smyrna
Laodicea
Colosse
Ephesus
Miletus
Rhodes
SCALE
1 50 100 150 200
MILES
Troas
THRACE
Neapolis
Aegean Sea
THE GREAT SEA
MEDITERRANEAN SEA
LIBYA
Philippi
Fair Havens
MOESIA
Thessalonica
Berea
Athens
Corinth
CRETE
DALMATIA
MACEDONIA
ACHAIA
Cyrene
Sea of Adria
Nicopolis
Ionian Sea
Syrtis Major
ITALY
Rhegium
Syracuse
TRIPOLIS
ROME
Etruscan Sea
SICILY
Melita

Bibliography

RESOURCES FOR FURTHER STUDY

Bruce, F. F. *The Letters of Paul: An Expanded Paraphrase.* Grand Rapids: Eerdmans, 1965.

Everyday Bible. New Testament Study Edition. Minneapolis: World Wide, 1988.

Jensen, Irving L. *How to Profit from Bible Reading.* Chicago: Moody, 1985.

_____. *Jensen's Survey of the New Testament.* Chicago: Moody, 1981.

Ryrie, Charles C. *Balancing the Christian Life.* Chicago: Moody, 1969.

Strong, James. *The Exhaustive Concordance of the Bible.* New York: Abingdon, 1890.

Tenney, Merrill C. *The Zondervan Pictorial Bible Dictionary.* Grand Rapids: Zondervan, 1963.

Unger, Merrill F. *New Unger's Bible Dictionary.* Chicago: Moody, 1988.

Vincent, Marvin R. *Word Studies in the New Testament.* Grand Rapids: Eerdmans, 1946.

Vine, W. C. *An Expository Dictionary of New Testament Words.* Westwood, N.J.: Revell, 1966.

COMMENTARIES AND TOPICAL STUDIES

Bruce, F. F. *1 and 2 Corinthians.* London: Oliphants, 1971.

Godet, Frederic L. *Commentary on First Corinthians.* Grand Rapids: Kregel, 1977.

Grosheide, F. W. *Commentary on the First Epistle to the Corinthians.* The New International Commentary on the New Testament. Grand Rapids: Eerdmans, 1953.

Johnson, S. Lewis. "First Corinthians." In *The Wycliffe Bible Commentary,* edited by Charles F. Pfeiffer and Everett F. Harrison. Chicago: Moody, 1962.

Kling, Christian Friedrich. "Corinthians." In *Commentary on the Holy Scriptures,* edited by John Peter Lange. Grand Rapids: Zonderan, n.d.

Lenski, R. C. H. *The Interpretation of St. Paul's First and Second Epistle to the Corinthians.* Columbus, Ohio: Wartburg, 1946.

Luck, G. Coleman. *First Corinthians.* Everyman's Bible Commentary. Chicago: Moody, 1958.

Morgan, G. Campbell. *The Corinthian Letters of Paul.* London: Oliphants, 1947.

Morris, Leon. *The First Epistle of Paul to the Corinthians.* Grand Rapids: Eerdmans, 1958.

Proctor, W. C. G. "1 Corinthians: Commentary." In *The New Bible Commentary,* edited by F. Davidson. Grand Rapids: Eerdmans, 1953.